D0976715

House
of
Steps

Also by Amy Blackmarr

Going to Ground

Amy Blackmarr

House of Steps

Finding the Path Home

Viking

VIKING
Published by the Penguin Group
Penguin Putnam Inc., 375 Hudson Street,
New York, New York 10014, U.S.A.
Penguin Books Ltd, 27 Wrights Lane, London W8 5TZ, England
Penguin Books Australia Ltd, Ringwood, Victoria, Australia
Penguin Books Canada Ltd, 10 Alcorn Avenue,
Toronto, Ontario, Canada M4V 3B2
Penguin Books (N.Z.) Ltd, 182–190 Wairau Road,
Auckland 10, New Zealand

Penguin Books Ltd, Registered Offices:
Harmondsworth, Middlesex, England

First published in 1999 by Viking Penguin,
a member of Penguin Putnam Inc.

1   3   5   7   9   10   8   6   4   2

Some of the selections in this book have been read on
Kansas's KCUR's "Up-to-Date" and Peach State Public
Radio's "Georgia Gazette."

Grateful acknowledgment is made for permission to reprint
"My Beard" from *Where the Sidewalk Ends* by Shel Silverstein.
Copyright © 1974 by Evil Eye Music, Inc. Used by permission
of HarperCollins Publishers.

LIBRARY OF CONGRESS CATALOGING-IN-PUBLICATION DATA
Blackmarr, Amy.
House of steps : finding the path home / Amy Blackmarr.
p.   cm.
ISBN 0-670-88237-2
1. McLouth Region (Kan.)—Social life and customs.
2. McLouth Region (Kan.)—Biography.   3. Country life—
Kansas—McLouth Region.   4. Blackmarr, Amy.   I. Title.
F689.M35B58   1999
978.1'37—dc21   98–53767

This book is printed on acid-free paper.
∞

Printed in the United States of America
Set in Stempel Schneidler
Designed by Betty Lew

To Joe Stofiel

Warm thanks to my agent, Lynn Nesbit;

my editors, Barbara Grossman and Amanda Patten,

and the talented Viking Penguin staff;

to Mom, Dad, Kelly, Joe, Deborah, John Hiers,

and Stephen Emerson Albright.

The world is its own magic.

Shunryu Suzuki

Contents

Contents

House

of

Steps

Prologue
Buzzard on the Bluff

*"Process": a continuing development involving
many changes; a method of doing something,
with all the steps involved*

Webster's New World Dictionary,
Warner Books Edition, 1987

*S*even years ago I promised myself I'd never again live a life
I didn't love. I sold my Kansas City paralegal business and
moved back down to South Georgia, where I grew up, to live
in my granddaddy's pond-side fishing cabin on our family
farm, and write. For five years I lived without hot water, was
too cold in winter and too hot in summer, and got to know
the mice and the water moccasins and the armadillos a little
too well—but I reveled in the certainty that I'd done exactly
the right thing. I was doing what I *wanted* to do: living in the
country, spending Saturdays with my grandmother MaRe
(short for *Ma*ma *Re*ba), and writing. I took in some dogs and
some cats. When I ran out of money, I went to college and
bought the groceries with government loans. I took biology
and history and trigonometry and kept writing.

During that time I wrote a bad Southern Gothic novel, a

mystery so tangled I never figured out how to end it, and a collection of purple meditations that now make me blush with embarrassment. I wrote a dozen poems and some children's stories. Then, writing columns for my southern university's newspaper, I discovered the personal essay. These grew into commentaries for public radio and, at last, a finished manuscript. To live by my writing: that was my other promise to myself.

Then came a surprise. I was offered a doctoral fellowship to study at the University of Kansas. Because the fellowship provided a living stipend for four years of writing, studying writing, and reading, I accepted. As it happened, my family had sold the farm after MaRe died, and I needed to move anyway.

But I didn't *want* to go back out West. Never mind that I'd lived in Kansas twelve years, married and divorced and made friends there; I'd reclaimed Georgia after years of trenchant disownership, and now I wanted to stay where the scents of pine straw on damp mornings and peanuts drying in October fields were deep and warm and familiar. I loved better the North Georgia cabin my Aunt Helen and Uncle Johnny had offered me, where I could see the Blue Ridge Mountains from the windows, and where the creeks ran cold and clear, and the accents still sounded like home.

But I did come back to Kansas, to these broad skies and incessant southerly winds that stream over the fields and bend down the long grasses like low-flying flocks of invisible birds. I came because it's where my promises brought me.

Now I live down fifteen miles of country roads near an

old northeastern Kansas rail town called McLouth, in a funky vision of a rental house built by a flower child as the 1960s faded. He was smoking the native ditchweed, I'm told, when he stopped measuring things like boards. What he ended up with is an M. C. Escher graphic that actually exists in all three dimensions and encloses a whirlwind of drafts.

I resented the place from the minute I saw it, as I stood on the winding gravel driveway with my little gray dog Max panting from the ungodly August heat and my truckload of belongings at my back. Out of urgency for a place to live, I'd signed the lease in Georgia based on three photographs and some phone conversations. But it wasn't what I'd imagined, this dark house with no rounded edges and little else that seemed to offer comfort. There was nothing soft or forgiving about it. It was a cobbled, ungainly affair that was not, after all, like something the Keebler Elves would live in. All yellow rock and brown frame, all blocks and angles and glaring window glass, it was a narrow contortion of plywood and limestone that strained upward over four levels and a tortuous profusion of stairs, straight into the tops of the chinkapin oaks and hickories. It was a house of steps, perched like a buzzard at the edge of a rocky bluff covered with scrappy hardwoods. The neighbors called it the Tree House.

But nearly two years have passed since I came back to Kansas, and the changes riding in on that troubled time have brought me around to understanding how, as the contemporary mystic Caroline Myss says, chaos is also God.

Returning to Georgia was my withdrawal from the world. Kansas has brought me back.

Today I sit in my study at the house of steps before the chapel window writing down those changes, peering at them from the angles my experience affords, and rediscover in every line the remarkable and incorruptible process of living from ordinary day to ordinary day. Today is Sunday. Early May. The doors are open and a southeast wind, strong and warm, is blowing the last traces of winter out of the house. The cottonwoods are greening. The sky is pale. The tattered irises some former tenant planted are blooming in the yard, and sweet blue phlox and wild violets cluster in the shade. The dogs lie on the deck in the sun, watching for wild turkeys to ramble up out of the woods.

Amy Blackmarr
Northeastern Kansas
May 15, 1998

House of Steps

"Two steps forward, one step back."

Psychologist, to patient
beginning long-term therapy

$\mathcal{G}$ood heavens, honey," said my genteel South Georgia mama as we stared up at the house of steps for the first time. "It's a hippie house."

It was August. Hot and steamy. Mom had followed me up from Georgia in my Honda; now she was helping me move in. I was standing next to her in cutoffs and a too-tight sports bra that made my chest feel pressed in, tying a bandanna around my head, getting ready to unload the U-Haul. The landlord, a small, dark-haired woman with a tentative smile, hovered beside her little red car, watching us. Max had trotted off to water things.

Mom cast a worried look back toward the road. "It's awfully remote," she said.

"I like remote," I said.

"You've definitely got remote," she said.

"It's not that remote," offered the landlord.

Remote wasn't what was bothering me. I was wondering how I'd keep that twisted driveway plowed in winter, that great upward stretch of house clean and the yard in shape (there was so much *more* of everything than I'd imagined), plus do research, write papers, write books, and commute fifteen miles to the university in Lawrence. Somehow, my phone conversations with my Kansas friend Sara, who'd been out to look the place over for me, hadn't quite prepared me for what I was seeing. "It has so much charm," she'd told me, "and a garden and lots of trees."

But right now, looking at a yard that seemed to meld with infinity, I was thinking about my humble red bargain of a push mower from Wal-Mart that was not self-propelled.

"Big yard," I said airily to the landlord.

"It's only half an acre," she answered.

"Why is there a bathtub in it?" Mom asked. She was looking at a big bathtub by the porch steps of a cedar shack, near some wild rosebushes.

"Oh, that's an outdoor sauna," said the landlord. "The tub is for . . . you know. Cooling off."

"I'll bet," said Mom.

We walked toward the sauna, past a low square of flat rocks that walled off a sizable garden, now overgrown with wild mustard and peppergrass. Rusty tomato cages were stacked in the corners. Wild mint covered the ground by the east wall, near a bird feeder on an eight-foot pole, and sage grew along the north wall among too many iris stalks. Bunches of giant foxtail grass were confined inside circles of fence wire along the west wall.

"What's this in the daisies?" I asked, noticing a small wooden cross near the garden. The name "Jesse," surrounded by flowers, was carved into the cross.

"That's a grave," said the landlord. "It's the former tenants' cat."

"It looks like a shrine," I said.

"To a cat?" said Mom.

"People like cats," I said.

"But it's right in the middle of the yard," said Mom.

"They wanted to know if they could visit it," said the landlord. "I told them it would be all right."

"It's not," I said.

"Amy, honey, if the landlord says—"

"Mom, just let me—"

"They wouldn't come in the house," explained the landlord.

I kicked a rock by the shrine.

Mom went to examine a square wooden post sunk into the ground. There were four of these, at varying heights. They formed a rough circle and leaned slightly inward, like a midwestern Stonehenge. "What are these things?" she asked.

"Those were part of the stage for the Climax Festival," said the landlord.

"The *what*?" said Mom.

"We had kind of a miniature Woodstock out here in the seventies," said the landlord.

"Ha," I said.

"Oh, my Lord," said my mother.

"Remember, I warned you," said the landlord as she let us in the bottom level of the house. "It's really neat inside, but it's rustic." She gave out a nervous laugh.

We stepped into the kitchen. I felt on my bare legs the current of drafts circulating over the brick floor and around the uninsulated rock walls. "It's like a cave in here," said Mom, running her hand over a wide window ledge, a gouged and stained wooden shelf that reminded me of an old cutting board I cleaned fish on at the cabin. She wrinkled her nose. "I wouldn't use this for anything that has to do with food," she said.

"It just needs washing, Mom."

"Oh, the house is clean," said the landlord quickly.

Mom turned on the water in the sink. A wolf spider darted out of the drain. "It's rustic, all right," she said.

"Mom, it's the *country*."

"Well, I can see what you like about it," she said, opening cabinets and peering inside. "It's like going to camp."

"I've been living in a tarpaper shack for five years without hot water," I bragged. "I can handle it."

"But that was South Georgia, honey. It *snows* in Kansas."

"We don't get that much snow," said the landlord.

"Snow is not a problem, Mother," I said. I fiddled with the knobs on the gas stove and looked in the oven. Out wafted a faint smell of rotten eggs. "Propane stove," I said.

Mom sniffed. "I wonder how old it is."

"I've never had any trouble with it," said the landlord.

Up a step off the kitchen was the only bathroom, barely wide enough for a tiny sink and, up another step, a toilet and an old tub. Air soughed in where the wall met the window. Mom ran her fingers around the window frame.

"The house has a few . . . quirks," said the landlord.

We walked around a corner past a pantry and up a steep, narrow staircase to the second floor. The stairs ended in a small room with a vaulted ceiling that dropped to three feet on the north side. A chapel window, facing an upward slope crowded with oaks and black walnut trees, covered most of the east wall. On the south side of the room, a stone hearth had once supported a woodstove. The exposed plywood subfloor, like the stairs, was painted with green porch paint.

Mom walked into the next room and came back. "There aren't any doors in this house," she said.

"That's one of the quirks," said the landlord.

"I like open spaces," I said.

Mom pulled at a hinged piece of plywood, looked behind it, and closed it again. "This looks like a crawl space," she said. "Where's the closet?"

"That's another one of the quirks," said the landlord.

"No closets?" asked Mom.

The landlord shrugged.

"Why would anybody build a house without closets?"

"Mom, I can live without closets."

"I'm glad," said Mom. "What is this?" She was looking at a triangle-shaped hole high up in one wall.

"Some kind of ventilation system, I think," said the landlord. "The guy who built this place left some things unfinished."

Mom shook her head. "This is the strangest house I've ever seen." She paused, then added, "He must have been an architecture student."

I decided to make this room my study.

The next room, which I called the den, was rounded, with wide windows, knotty pine ceilings, green floors, and either six or eight walls, depending on how we counted. No two walls were the same width. I opened the sliding glass door, which led onto a deck with built-in benches and eleven steps down to the yard. The bird feeder was nearby. An ancient redbud tree grew up through a hole in the deck.

"This is nice, Mom," I said, looking out. Max lay on his stomach in a patch of shade under a basswood tree. The wooded bluff was to my left, which was south, the driveway to my right. West, beyond the garden, the yard merged with a grassy meadow dotted with red cedars and knots of sumac. This property was only a few acres, I knew, but it seemed to link up on every side with vacant land. The landlord had said there were neighbors, but they must be a long way from here.

From the den we climbed a steep spiral of open steps with no railing, which presented a breathtaking view when we looked down from the top landing.

"Whoooo," said Mom. "Vertigo."

"Mom—"

"Oh, look, Amos. Here's the other end of the triangle." It was at the top of the stairs. She put her head into the opening. "Hellooooo," she said. "Anybody in there?"

"Mother," I said. "Good grief."

The third floor was a single small room shaped like a long octagon, a kind of lookout tower that seemed to float among the treetops. Windows went all the way around, facing every approach. There were clear views across the yard to the meadow and down the driveway. South- and eastward was a sea of waving green, the tops of sycamores, cottonwoods, hickories, and locusts. The ground was forty feet down.

"This'll be a great place to sleep," I said.

"It's an awfully long way to the bathroom," said Mom.

"I'll get used to it," I said. "Hey." I noticed a set of folding stairs in the ceiling. "There's another floor up here."

"That's the attic," said the landlord.

I grabbed the cord to pull down the stairs.

"You might not want to do that," said the landlord, backing up a step.

"I want to see what's up there."

"Amy, honey, if the landlord says not to—"

"Stand back, Mom." I yanked the cord.

"Look out!" Mom shouted, waving her arms at the contingent of wasps that dive-bombed us from the attic.

I let the cord go and the staircase slammed shut.

"I was going to say," said the landlord, "that you might want to be holding a can of hornet spray when you open that."

After the landlord left with my rent money in her pocket, Mom disappeared into the kitchen, and I backed the U-Haul up to the deck steps and lay the ramp on the third step from the bottom. This meant I only had to carry my truckload of belongings up the eight steps left to the den, or down the hill and around the corner to the kitchen. At the moment, I was glad I'd been doing my Buns of Steel workout with hand weights.

I opened the trailer doors and sighed at the crammed accumulation of my adult years—mostly books, a few chairs, the coffee mugs and kitchen appliances that seemed to proliferate on their own. My bike. My computer. A TV and some lamps. Where would I put it all? This place seemed so complicated, with its mazy turns and stairs and drafts and driveway that needed shoveling in winter. Life at Pop's cabin had been so simple. One huge room, a handful of spiders and lizards, a few snakes and some mice. An old boat against a pine tree, and a straight line of sight from Monday to Sunday.

What flashed through my memory was my first wedding in MaRe's yard when I was seventeen, how I had a chance

to back out as I stood on the patio in my wedding dress looking doubtfully at the ivy-garlanded gazebo, the groom in
his morning coat and ascot, the bridesmaids in their green
velvet chokers and ivory gowns, the gladiolus sprays tied
with white satin, the murmuring onlookers in their Sunday
clothes. When I took my dad's arm to start down the aisle, I
burst into tears. Daddy, alarmed, patted my hand. "Is everything all right, Sweetie Pie?" he said. But determination having never been a quality I lacked, I just sighed and began our
procession. It seemed the only thing to do at the time.

"Just wait till you see this place! It's like a storybook
house!" I'd told my friends down South, flashing my three
photos of the house of steps. "It's got birds and a creek and
all these trees!"

"Is Kansas got trees, Amy?" my neighbor Gene asked.
"That don't look like Kansas to me."

🏠 Next day, as the afternoon crept toward sunset, my
books towered in unsteady stacks along the den walls, next
to the boxes of steel shelves I was avoiding. I'd spent the
morning putting one together in the pantry, clutching the
frame between my feet while I balanced a shelf above my
head with one hand and screwed down bolts with the other.
At critical moments I'd call for help, and Mom would come
in and hold things. With both of us jammed into that airless
inner room that still reeked of, I presume, Him to whom the
shrine was erected in the yard, we found ourselves twist-
ing around each other in shapes I'd forgotten bodies could

make. All that was missing was the big colored dots on the floor. "Right foot, blue! Left hand, yellow!" It might have been a parody of my adolescence, except then we weren't laughing.

Now a mizzling rain was making the paint bubble on the bookcases that Mom had painted the color of eggshells and left on the deck to dry, and the heat was torpid. She was in the kitchen, organizing my too many pots and pans, and I was traipsing across the deck, down the steps, over the ramp, and into the U-Haul, shouldering the last of my stuff. I dropped a final armload of computer cables onto the pile in the middle of the den and dug through the boxes to find a light bulb for the lamp.

The bulb found, and the lamp, shadeless, turned on to light the deepening dusk inside, I went back out to lock the U-Haul for the night. The drizzle was letting up. The wind was warm. Fireflies drifted over the yard along the line of trees to the south, and I leaned against the truck cab and watched them, and listened to the cicadas, and breathed in the fragrance of rich earth beneath damp grass. You can grow anything in this soil, somebody had told me.

After a while, Mom called me in for supper, and for a moment I heard an old lullaby sound in her voice and felt an extraordinary tenderness for her, and it made me a child again, as if all the difficult years of getting from one part of my life to the next, and the difficult days of moving from one place to the next, had rolled back, leaving before me only a friendly, unwritten space.

Well, at least, I thought, at least there's that.

I whistled for Max, and he came rustling through the underbrush from some far point in the woods. When I turned back to the house, the single lamplight was glowing yellow behind the many curtainless windows, casting into the yard pale paths like stories that stretched outward at every angle until they faded into the distance.

Mowing

It's all interpretation.

Diamond Rio

$\mathcal{I}$n the M. C. Escher graphic "Ascending and Descending," steps on a parapet make a square. Knights go down and around the steps, passing knights going up and around. The going-up knights always go up, but they never go any higher: they only go around and around. The going-down knights always go down but never go lower: they just go around, too. I know this is an illusion, but I can't see where the trick is.

In this yard, I'm a going-up knight.

I knew I'd have a yard to mow in Kansas, so before I left Georgia I bought a push mower on sale at the Wal-Mart. Not the kind without an engine—I'm not into self-punishment, even if I do like a challenge.

("Why do you always do things the hard way?" a friend asked me once.

"Because if I didn't, I wouldn't be living up to my potential."

"According to whom?")

My lawn mower was fire-engine red. *Zoom, zoom,* I thought. With a little effort, my mower can tackle anything in Kansas.

It rained for three weeks after I moved to the house of steps, and by the time the sun came out and the yard seemed dry enough to mow, the grass was a foot high. So on a Sunday afternoon after lunch, which is the proper time for yard work, I donned my armor—running shorts, sports bra, tennis shoes with double-tied laces—and went outside to try my new lawn mower. Never mind that the thermometer I'd nailed up on the deck read ninety-five and when I stepped outside the air slapped me in the face like wet laundry. I was a South Georgia girl. I'd grown up where breathing made you sweat.

I went under the deck, slid the shiny machine out of the box, and read the directions. Max watched from under a tree.

"Wear leather shoes," said the directions. "Do *not* wear tennis shoes. In case you back up over your feet."

Egad, I thought. How could you run over your own feet?

"Wear long pants," said the directions.

In this weather? Forget that.

I tightened bolts and screws, poured in gas and oil, connected the spark plug wire, and fired up the engine. No problem. *Varoom, varoom.* Look at me, I thought. I'm so independent.

Already soaked with sweat, I rolled off toward the sauna.

Or rather, I shoved off, through still-damp grass that was thicker than it looked. Max trotted behind me and chased the disinherited frogs.

Down the straightaway I rattled. Shove, shove over the thick patches. Push, push around the first turn. Piece of cake. Shove, shove. *Thunk.*

An invisible hole under the grass swallowed the mower's front wheels and wouldn't let go. I yanked and the machine lurched backward. It landed an inch shy of my tennis shoes.

I realigned the mower and shoved forward. Bump, bump, bump. *Thunk.* Yank, realign, shove. *Thunk.* Good grief.

Shove. *Thunk.*

Shove. *Thunk.*

I stopped and looked around. I could see now that there were mole runs everywhere, a whole half-acre network of tunnels where moles had pushed up the grass in soft ridges that grabbed the mower and jerked it to a stop.

Max caught a mole once. I brought it in the house and played with it on a towel. It was gray-brown with velvety fur and about the size of a field mouse, and it made squeaking noises when I touched it. Its eyes wouldn't open and its feet were webbed like small spatulas, for digging speed bumps in your yard.

I headed south, cutting around the trunks of the rough-leaf dogwoods and under the thorny branches of the hedge-apple trees. Bumpity-bump. *Bam.*

A wide, flat rock, hidden in the grass, jutted out of the ground.

Okay, I thought, so the yard is an obstacle course and this isn't easy. So what?

Max rolled in the cut grass and crawled under the sauna.

I pushed on, rattling over a shady patch where the lawn was so thin, the mower peppered my bare legs with Lilliputian arrows and bullets of dirt. Then I shoved along the tree line, where I had to bend over every few steps to pick up sticks or avoid overhanging limbs.

But I could use a little waist action, I thought, glancing down at where my middle folded out from under the band of my sports bra. I could hear the drill sergeant in my head, the one that makes me work out on my NordicTrack at midnight. "All right, you slacker! Show some hair! Move it, now! Mow! Mow! Stop! Bend! Twist! Straighten! Mow!"

I turned the corner and headed for the burn-barrel by the driveway, and *I* didn't stop but the mower did and I got a smart right hook in the abdomen when I almost flipped headfirst over the handle. It reminded me of that day in 1963 when Sherry Cumby and I were riding bikes around the tennis court at the end of the alley behind my house. I and my new blue Western Flyer went speeding through a mid-net gap that turned out to be a steel cable. The bike stopped and I kept going.

This time, the lawn mower ground to a halt and wouldn't budge. It wasn't a hill so much as a mild slope, but it was thick with shin-high grass that had choked down the engine. I pulled the cord to restart it and managed to advance a few inches. Again the mower died. Again I started the engine, leaned into it with all my strength and, almost horizontal with the effort, pushed ahead.

🏠After an hour in tropical heat my mind was a blank slate and I still had a long way to go. When I moved, the chiggers crawled under my waistband, and when I stood still, the flies bit me. I was sure I could feel three ticks on my head. I'd had enough.

I didn't even put the mower away, just left it by the spigot, where it sputtered out of gas, and plodded back to the house, squinting against the reflections of afternoon sun in the windows.

I poured a glass of tea, then came back and flopped down on the deck steps like a dead fish. My shoulders ached from strain and my face from sunburn. My hands were blistered and stuck to my work gloves. My knees were so weak they quaked.

I looked out on the peculiar geometry of my effort. I'd left no neat lines anywhere, having steered around cat shrine, trees, sauna, garden wall, burn-barrel, spigot, mole runs, and sudden outcroppings of rock.

🏠When I moved in, the landlord told me I didn't have to mow the whole yard. "Do as much or as little as you want," she said.

But the tenants before me cut a wide path through the

meadow all the way to the creek. They kept the weeds trimmed along the driveway and mowed around the wood-pile behind the sauna. So what if they'd had a tractor and all I had was a push mower: they'd set the standard. I couldn't do less. I'm a going-up knight. I wear armor, and I go up and up and up.

The Wasp Lady and
the Red Porsche

*H*enry David Thoreau didn't trouble himself about the wasps that settled in his Walden cabin. He thought they were paying him a compliment, keeping company with him, climbing between his bedcovers and hanging out by the windows. But then wild birds sat on Thoreau's shoulder, and loons led him on chases across the pond, and mice ate out of his hands. So maybe wasps didn't sting Thoreau, because if they had, he might not have liked them so well.

Over my bed, eight green pine-scented garbage bags that I taped over the cracks around the attic staircase billow in the heat that wafts upward from the floor vent. I put the bags up in September, after I'd killed my fiftieth wasp in a single day.

A wasp may be ponderous but he's hard as the limestone in my Kansas driveway. Flyswatters only annoy him. If I cut off his back half with a letter opener, his front half buzzes around on the windowsill all day. The only way to kill him is to squash him with my shoe. So today I'm on the lookout for the wasp lady, who is on the way over to spray something lethal in the attic.

"Alls you need is one application," she'd told me. "That's all the more it takes. Stuff works forever."

"Forever! What is it? Should I breathe?"

"You can breathe," she said. "After a couple hours."

"Good Lord. Is it nerve gas or something?"

"Diatomaceous earth."

"Is that some kind of dirt?"

"An abrasive. You know how wasps is always cleaning theirselves? Well, they walk around in this stuff and it gets on their little feet. Then when they rub it on theirselves, they scrape off their waterproof coating and dehydrate."

"But that's a horrible way to die!"

"Yeah."

I was wondering about my waterproof lungs, but when the woman showed up in Desert Storm fatigues holding a blowtorch, I decided not to ask.

A wasp biologist I know tells me I should make friends with the wasps. "Wasps are necessary," she says. "Anyway, what about your reverence for life?"

A kendo master asked me the same question when he read about the snakes I'd tried to shoot back in Georgia.

"Guilty of self-contradiction," I say, and to soften the impression of me as a cold-blooded killer I tell how I cringe when I slam into the frogs that leap out in front of my speeding car on spring nights or when I beat the lettuce on the kitchen counter to loosen the core. What I don't tell about is the time I volunteered for the army.

"You're off the charts in field artillery and combat arms," said the puzzled recruiter as he examined my test results.

"I told you," I said. "I want to jump out of airplanes. Put me in combat training."

"We don't let women in combat training," he said. (It was the unenlightened eighties.)

Turned out I was too nearsighted anyway.

When I lived in Kansas in my twenties, I rented an apartment in the Kansas City suburbs. Having grown up in an area of Georgia so rural you had to drive twenty miles to see a movie, I never found city living easy on my senses, but my concrete patio in Overland Park was divided from suburban noisiness by two mulberry trees and a tall wooden fence. On summer days when a southwest breeze was up, the rustle of mulberry leaves and the songs of the robins in the nearby pin oaks covered over the sound of cars going by on the street, and maybe the air smelled a little like the lake eight miles away, and I could sit in my lawn chair and imagine I was in the country.

On just that sort of day, on Labor Day weekend, I was sitting in the lawn chair with my feet propped up on the steps, reading a book, when a fat red squirrel came tripping along the fence ledge, which was several inches wide. All at once he plopped down on his stomach and, balancing on the ledge, let his front and back legs dangle. There he lay for the longest time, looking sleepy.

Astonished, and fighting an urge to uncross my feet for fear of startling him, I watched him until his eyes closed. Then my toes started going numb and I had to move, and the squirrel woke up and dashed away.

Right after that a roach crawled over my foot, and I gasped and shook him off and then burst out laughing because when I lifted my foot to squash him I found I couldn't do it, couldn't break that thread that ran through the roach and the squirrel and me and the robins and the mulberry tree.

My friend Joe once explained that people have contradictory ideas of themselves on different days. "It's like you're made up of a dozen spark plugs that all fire at different times," he said, drawing a diagram for me on a piece of paper. "Every spark plug is a different idea. One day you drive through town in a red Porsche and wear glitter on your eyelids. The next day you live in a monastery and don't like men."

On my red Porsche days, I murder wasps and try to join the army. On monastery days, I fall into ecstasies over roaches.

Black Widow, Brown Spider

$\mathcal{I}$ never saw so many spiders in my life," I said to the stove man, who had come to stop the propane leak that was making the house smell like unfound Easter eggs. "Even in Georgia, in the *tropics,* we don't have spiders like this. You could use these spiders for golf balls."

"Come on, now," said the stove man, a blond, angular fellow, pulling the stove out from the wall.

"You could," I said, looking at him. "They ambush you."

The stove man sniffed, then bent down and put his hand on the propane pipe. "You got a leak," he said.

"Like highway robbers."

"It needs cleaned back here."

"They hang out in the trees at night," I went on. "If you

walk around without a flashlight, they jump on you. Big old fat things. I'd hate to step on one."

"Carry a stick and wave it in front of you," said the stove man, fumbling for a tool in his toolbox. "What you got here is a problem."

"Don't tell me. Tell the landlord."

"I can fix it," he said, pounding on the pipe. "What you got to watch out for is those brown recluse spiders. I knew a boy got a brown spider bite on the inside of his thigh took a year to heal. Made a big hole in his leg."

"I heard they get in your shoes," I said.

"Get behind the furniture, too. Get in your folded clothes." He stood up and pushed the stove back against the wall. "That ought to do it." He leaned against the sink and started writing out the bill. "I caught a black widow in a jar once when I was seven," he said.

"You didn't!"

"Caught it with some other spiders. I put the jar on the porch and then forgot about it for two months. When I went back to check on it, everything was dead except the black widow."

"She killed all the other ones?"

"Or they died of starvation. Well, I opened that jar and then took off running. Just ran and ran. Ran for a block and a half. But every time I looked behind me, that spider was right there."

"Where?"

"Right there behind me."

"No!"

"Every time I looked around."

"But that's impossible. How could that be?"

He shook his head. "Scared me so bad, to this day I'm still terrified of spiders."

"Must make it hard for you," I said, "crawling around behind stoves all the time."

"Well, I just keep my eyes open and"—here he paused and raised an eyebrow at me—"I try not to think about spiders much."

"Ohhhh," I said. "So how do you like our Jayhawks this year?"

The fall afternoon had turned warm, and I was reaching up to pull back the blanket that I'd hung over the chapel window to stop the draft from blowing on my head at night when my palm suddenly felt like it had been pierced with the tip of a hot knife. I drew my hand back and gazed at it, stunned, and saw a red dot quickly becoming surrounded by a ring of bloodless skin a quarter inch wide.

Brown spider bite. *Brown spider bite!* I thought.

I knew it was a brown spider bite because of what the stove man had said, about brown spiders hiding in your folded clothes.

Anyway I had the evidence right before my eyes, because my hand was already starting to turn white from lack of circulation. Soon it would die and start to rot. Brown spider bites make you rot. Everybody knows that.

I paced the den floor and cradled my throbbing hand. I'd heard that meat tenderizer might break down the poison, but I didn't have any meat tenderizer, though I'd put it on my grocery list often enough, for treating insect bites.

But I did have baking soda, and it had helped a yellow jacket sting once. I ran downstairs to the kitchen and made a baking-soda paste and put it over the bite.

Now my hand was going numb, except for occasional shooting pains.

It *would* have to be my right hand, I thought. How will I write? I'll have to learn to type one-handed.

Maybe I could hire a transcriptionist, I thought. I could be like Milton. Milton was blind. I'd be handless.

I called Sara and asked her what to do. "Emergency!" I shouted into the phone. "I've been bitten by a brown spider!"

"You should get to a doctor," she said. "Can you drive?"

"No." (My Honda has a stick shift.) "I'm scared to death."

"Sit tight. I'll come take you to the emergency room."

"Unfortunately," said Dr. Rock, frowning as he poked my palm with his finger, "this is all muscle here and it's pretty close to the bone. If it becomes necrotic, there's no way to stop it."

"What do you mean, no way to stop it?" I yelled. "What about amputation?"

"Not even that."

"Agghh! But that doesn't make sense."

"I know," said Dr. Rock. "Nobody understands it. But if the necrosis reaches the bone, well . . ."

"Don't tell me," I said. "It's too ugly."

Dr. Rock patted me on the shoulder. "Now, don't you start worrying yet. Just keep an eye on this hand and let's see what's happening Thursday." He wrote out a prescription for antibiotics and gave me some Tylenol.

Sara drove me to her house, where I, in a throbbing stupor, sat at the kitchen table resting my hand palm-up on my knee while I watched her eat chili because she was starved from missing her supper.

How can she eat like that when I'm sitting here with my hand rotting off? I was thinking.

The next day, depressed, I called my botanist friend, who makes field trips into the wilderness all the time.

"That doesn't sound like a brown recluse to me," he said. "Do you have wasps out there?"

"Are you kidding? I killed fifty last Tuesday."

"Because that sounds like a wasp sting to me. They hurt like that. Brown recluse bites don't work that fast."

"Huh," I said. "You've got to be kidding."

"Did you see what bit you?"

"Well, no. I just assumed . . ."

"Why didn't you call me sooner?" he said. Then he

described the symptoms of a wasp sting, which I ticked off one by one.

By Thursday my hand didn't hurt any more, and I canceled my appointment with Dr. Rock and made one with the wasp lady instead.

A Surprise in the Forest

It is the unknown that defines our existence. We are explorers.

> Commander Benjamin Sisko,
> *Deep Space 9*

$\mathcal{I}$t was late September and Max had already made paths. One narrow trail through the yard led to the spigot, where I kept his bucket of water. A second angled from the spigot to under the sauna, where he got out of the sun. A third snaked through the foxtail grass beside the driveway to a tiny pond, where he barked at minnows. A fourth wound down the bluff and into the woods behind the house, disappearing into regions unknown.

Max had no trouble settling in. He watered everything as soon as he got here and then trotted off to examine the neighborhood cows and assert his superiority over the local roughnecks—all of them big, furry, soft kinds of dogs compared to the feist-like, hard-bodied, bobcat-fighting, bowlegged Max, with the one ear that flops forward like a wilted petunia.

I, on the other hand, still felt dispossessed, like a Faulkner character in a cowboy song. One minute I was standing on the back steps of a Georgia cabin, drinking sweet tea and watching the light play over the pond—and then I was gone, swept up in a current of choices that set me down on a hard patch of midwestern ground to which I'd never expected to return. The world was certainly, as Carson McCullers wrote, a sudden place.

Now I was looking west out the den window feeling like an unmoored boat, noticing how in the woods behind the house the underbrush was finally beginning to die back. I wanted to learn the character of this land, feel how it rose and fell under my feet, find a connection to it. I missed walking, missed the miles of old logging roads that led from Pop's cabin through the pines and cotton fields down to the swamp. From the house of steps, there seemed nowhere to go. The long dirt road to the blacktop was a narrow linked chain of blind curves and low hills where the cars flew too fast down loose gravel, on the point of overturning.

But maybe now that the woods were thinning some, I could hike back there without stepping on timber rattlers, which my neighbor Skip said I should keep watch for. They like to stretch out in those cool, shallow caves under the bluffs, he told me. (They also like to stretch out in my driveway, I discovered, and in the woodpile behind the sauna.)

It was a blustery morning not quite cool enough for a sweater. I pulled on my paint-spattered jeans and high-top boots, took down my South Carolina hickory walking stick from where it had hung by the den door since the day I moved in, and struck off with Max down his path into the woods. The trail angled southwest and crossed a dry branch that we traced to a wheat-colored clearing dotted with purpletop, sumac, wild senna, and tawny prairie grasses whose names I didn't know, that nodded and bowed under the unsteady wind. Without the trees to filter it, the light in the clearing was brittle and I squinted, and occasionally the wind brought the sound of a truck going by on the road, throwing up dust and sending the gravel flying. A red-tailed hawk flew over, keening. Ahead of me, Max vanished into a profusion of goldenrod and brown-eyed Susans. I followed and soon found a creek.

The creek bed was five or six paces across, but the water was shallow as it trickled over the limestone that's scattered over a large part of the eastern Kansas landscape. The ground here was damp and carpeted with plantain and purple lobelia, thorny blackberry vines, and wild pea plants that looked like miniature mimosas. I found wild onion by the smell, and bee balm leaves I could use to make tea.

It was strange how the land where I was walking didn't conform at all to my childhood notions of Out West. Northeastern Kansas isn't flat, glaring expanses of prairie and grassy bluffs, but green valleys, and wide stretches of corn and soy beans and sunflowers tall as Amazons, and rivers—the Kansas, the Delaware, the Wakarusa—banked by cottonwoods and gray and yellow rock.

But only a short drive west, on the far side of Topeka, the land levels out and the trees scatter and the ground starts sloping upward, and an airplane heading from here to Denver at twenty-five hundred feet above sea level would fly into the ground at Goodland, Kansas, on the western border. That's the Out West of Dodge City and Great Bend, of *Gunsmoke* and White Woman Creek, where the luminescent wheat ranges over endless fields and all you can see on the horizon is a straight, treeless edge of land, and the hills swell up out of the ground and roll toward Colorado like waves, and if you live around Hays or WaKeeney or Colby you can stand on your front porch and watch a car coming down a dusty road for miles. The occasional creeks that score the prairies are afterthoughts scraped out of the earth with a rusty trowel. Wisps of cloud trail across pale skies over a land of scorched yellows, tans, and browns, and washed blues and greens. It's a long way between houses out there, each solitary structure inside its clump of windbreak trees in the center of a vast plain. "Once you cross a land like that," wrote the Kansas poet William Stafford, "you own your face more. Every rock denies all the rest of the world."

But there where I was walking, things weren't so far apart, and hiking east down Max's trail in this valley now I squinted at the trees, searching for glimpses of other houses near the house of steps. I was curious about the people who would live out here in this untamed country, in houses you couldn't see from the road. I thought they must be eccentric, like me, and fiercely independent, like me. Maybe even a little dangerous. I was thinking I'd turn and follow the creek back in the other direction, to see if I could find any of their houses and spy on them from behind.

A track through the grass was keeping roughly parallel

to the creek. It had been driven on recently—the grass was flattened—and I found a half-dozen beer cans and a bed of dead coals. I listened but didn't hear anybody, but I was thinking: *Poachers*. I'm always worrying about poachers. Living in out-of-the-way places for so many years I've heard their trucks prowling the woods at odd hours, seen their flashlights in the dark, found their traps.

I called to Max and we hiked on, but I was wary. Max took frequent side trips to sniff around and mark territory.

After a while, I spotted a rusty barrel overturned on the creek bank. I wondered how it got there, and what might be inside, so I crept around to look. I didn't know what I thought I'd find, but I'll admit that the idea of body parts did occur to me. I'm always imagining grisly fingers and disembodied heads poking out of the dirt, or ghostly forms flitting among the trees. Too many Edgar Allan Poe stories when I was little, I guess. Too many séances and Ouija boards, and dark nights hunting through graveyards.

So I was disappointed to find only a few nondescript bottles, empty, and some plastic bags and roaches. I poked around with my walking stick, but nothing else turned up.

I was about to go on when I glanced to my left and noticed, at the top of a low bluff maybe fifty paces away, a large concrete box set into the hillside under some walnut trees—no, two concrete boxes, one slightly above the other. I couldn't see any openings in them, but maybe they had doors on the other side. This was strange.

I thought: *Moonshine*. Growing up in Georgia, you're always on the lookout for old stills in the woods.

I sneaked up the hill, searching for an entrance, listening for watchdogs or alarms or footsteps. "Max!" I whispered. "Get over here!" He was crashing around in the underbrush like revenuers on a raid.

Then a terrible idea struck me: *What if somebody is locked up in there?* I was picturing Grace Poole in *Jane Eyre,* trapped in a dark corner of Rochester's house, moaning and insane. Frankenstein's monster chained to a lab table. Neglected children in moldy basements. I spied a rusty handle on the lower box, and I tiptoed forward to examine it. Max was a few feet away, watching me.

All at once a gust of wind blew through the trees near the top of the bluff, and behind the parting branches I glimpsed a dark house, half hidden. It had an aspect of wariness, like a lookout at the start of his watch, and its windows glinted like searchlights through the chattering leaves.

That's definitely hand-built, I thought. *What a spooky place. These people are weird.* I imagined narrow-eyed, gaunt-faced ghouls peeping at me from the windows, with chains rattling around their shoulders, and heaps of bones on the kitchen table.

Then suddenly I thought: *What if somebody's home?*

In a panic, I whispered, "Go, Max!" and started to turn back . . . but just then I caught sight of a weathered shack in the yard. I inched closer and craned my neck to see better. A car was parked nearby. It looked like—I could barely see the top of it—it was a Honda. A green Honda.

Hey, I thought. *They have a car just like mine.*

A few more steps and I could see something big and

white in the yard beside the shack. A bathtub. There was a bathtub in the yard.

Hey, wait a minute, I thought. *That looks like . . .*

Uh-oh.

🏠 My dad likes to quote Pogo to me. His favorite line is "We have met the enemy, and it is us."

That *was* my Honda.

And that battered shack was an old hippie's sauna, complete with outdoor bathtub, and those concrete boxes were nothing but old cisterns. Made obsolete by a water line, they held neither moonshine nor madwomen, but only dust.

That looming shadow of a house was none other than the house of steps.

And the weird people who lived there?

They were me.

I climbed on up the bluff, laughing so hard I could hear myself echoing all the way down the valley.

Striking Out; or, It's Just Kids

$\mathcal{I}$t was near midnight on a Sunday and I was curled up in pajamas in my big brown chair in the den, watching the sexually frustrated Jane Tennyson set another prime suspect free. In this *Mystery!* episode, a boy had set his Dobermans on another boy in an empty swimming pool.

The den windows were open, letting in a stiff breeze that blew back the Mexican blanket I'd hung over the study doorway. Max was asleep on the floor.

After a while, I began to realize that other voices, men's voices, were entering my awareness beneath the sound of the TV. I hit the mute button and sat up, listening. Men were talking in the woods. They were aggressive and loud. They sounded drunk. Max looked up and growled.

The words were unintelligible, slung together in long

exclamatory fragments. There was laughter, then yelling. Laughter and hooting and yelling. I thought: *Sounds like trouble.*

I paced the floor and took inventory, trying to think how to stay safe. I didn't have a gun. I did have a can of Mace Mom had bought at the Wal-Mart despite my protests, and there was an old hunting knife in the basket by the bed.

I found the Mace in a drawer and set it down on the floor beside the chair.

I was imagining cases of beer iced down in the beds of pickups and shotguns racked across back windows. Oily hands and dirty jokes. Maybe it was the stories of beatings and burnings from the year I'd spent volunteering at the battered women's shelter, and that one woman in the hospital bed next to mine when I had my appendectomy, whose husband had run over her with his car. Or maybe there's some primal fear of men—of rape or domination—that all women carry with them. I don't know. But this late at night, alone, on the outskirts of civilization with those rude voices outside, I felt like a virgin trapped on a dark wharf with a boatload of sea-worn sailors rowing in.

Max barked and went to the den door. I couldn't get him quiet. The last thing I needed was to draw attention to a presence here, to the suggestive fact of the solitary car in the driveway.

I turned off the lights and climbed the stairs to the tower to look through the south windows. The moon was bright, but even with my binoculars I couldn't see anyone—at least not in the woods.

The voices sounded closer now, and more distinct; I counted five.

I called Skip, but he said he couldn't hear anything. "There was a big tractor pull in town tonight," he said. "It's probably just kids."

"How comforting," I said.

I called the sheriff. The dispatcher told me the deputy was working a road accident and would get to my place as soon as he could. I begged her not to send him down to the house. "Tell him to drive along the road," I said, "and find out what it is and call me."

I watched the rest of *Prime Suspect* with the sound turned low and the voices from outside drifting into the house and Max trotting back and forth, back and forth, back and forth in front of the door.

Half an hour passed and still no deputy. I turned off the TV and tiptoed around the rooms, looking out the windows. If only I could *see* them, I thought. If I just knew what they were *doing*.

Impatient, and tired of waiting, I grabbed my walking stick—I forgot about the Mace—locked Max in the house, and strode up the pale swath of driveway in the moonlight.

I couldn't tell where the voices were coming from. I'd thought they were south of the house; now they sounded northeast. When I reached the little pond beside the driveway, I counted again. One, two, three, four, five. Five male voices.

No, wait. A sixth voice. A woman's laugh. I stood still, trying to puzzle out how she fit in with the drunken men.

A car was creeping down the gravel road. At the top of the driveway, it stopped.

I froze.

Then I realized. It was the deputy. I waved my flashlight at him. When he saw me, he got out of his car. "The dispatcher said you didn't want me to go down there to your house," he said.

"I didn't."

He looked at my flashlight, my walking stick. "Where were you going to?"

"I got impatient."

He hitched his shoulders. "It's your neighbors to the south," he said. "They had a party after the tractor pull."

"Oh, no. My *neighbors*?"

"I know all those boys, and I went over there and told them to take it inside. If they don't quieten down, you call me back." He gave me his card.

Great, I thought. Now I've called the sheriff on my neighbors. When you live in the country, the last thing you want to do is make enemies of your neighbors. "Out here sometimes the only law you got's your thirty-eight," a neighbor told me once.

"You didn't tell them who called, I hope," I said.

"No, ma'am."

"I feel terrible."

I was remembering when I lived in an apartment and my neighbors called the police on me, and I'd get a knock on my door late at night. "We've had a complaint about the loud music," the officer would say, looking suspiciously past me into the room. "Why didn't they just ask me?" I'd say, embarrassed.

"This is awful, just awful," I told the deputy. "They'll never forgive me."

"It's this wind, coming across the valley," he said, "what makes it sound so close."

The following weekend, long past midnight, I was lying in bed, unable to sleep. The moon was still up, and it cast shadows through the uncurtained windows, spilling the dark shapes of trees down the walls and across the floor. The wind was out of the north, bringing infrequent truck sounds from the road. Max was curled up in the brown chair, asleep.

I'd been listening to a distant truck approaching for some time. Now it was coming around the curve up the hill. Near the top of the driveway it stopped, idling. Why didn't it go on by?

Max growled.

Male voices rose over the rumble of the engine.

Suddenly I heard banging, like metal on metal, and shouts and coarse laughter. Max ran to the den door, barking. I lay rigid, listening.

I tried to think what to do. What if they were coming to the house? Maybe I should call the sheriff again. But I was too scared to move.

Truck doors slammed. Between Max's barks, I heard

yelling and more banging. More doors slammed. Tires spun. A loud "WHOOOOO!" followed the sound of the truck careening down the road.

Stiff and straight, fists clenched, I waited to see if it would come back.

Max got quiet. After a while I heard him jump back up in the chair.

Watching the shadows move along the walls as the minutes passed, I remembered a night at the cabin in Georgia when some juveniles broke out of a maximum-security prison and fled down the cabin road. After they defecated in my neighbor Gene's driveway and wiped themselves with a shirt, which they left on a tree stump as a calling card, they stole the three-wheeler out of his barn. But they had to ditch it because they couldn't get it started. The next day, I could see their footprints in the sand by my front gate, my dogs, no doubt, having scared them away with the barking that had awakened me. Two days later, the sheriff caught them. They'd been in jail for car theft and aggravated assault. "Kids today," said the deputy, shaking his head, when he came to give me the news.

The next morning was sunny and warm. I walked up the drive looking for tire tracks and found them. The tires were wide and knobby. Flattened grass and broken sumac showed where the truck had turned around near the pond, and it had left deep ruts as it spun back up the steep hill to the road.

I followed the ruts to the mailbox. Now I understood the banging. The mailbox was lying on the ground beside the post. On the box's left side, a dirty boot print showed where it had been kicked in. Other dents suggested a club or a hammer. The box was gaping open, so misshapen it was impossible to close. I looked inside. The bills I'd left the night before to be picked up by the mailman that morning, the bills with checks—they were gone.

My first thought: It's the neighbors. They're getting back at me for calling the law on their party.

I'd never heard of this popular teenage sport the deputy called "baseball mailbox"—later corrected by my cousin to "mailbox baseball," which made only slightly more sense.

"What makes all that noise, they use aluminum bats," said the deputy. "If they can knock it off the post, it's a home run. A dent like you got would be first base."

"That sounds like a high school date," I said.

He shrugged and looked apologetic. He bent over the hood of his car, where he scribbled notes on a vandalism report form. From the back seat, the biggest German shepherd I'd ever seen was snarling at Max, who was taking care to pee on all the tires. The police dog's name was Max, too, only on his card (he had his own business cards) the name was spelled *MAXX*.

"The thing that gets me," I told the deputy, "it's so violent. What would I do if they came down to the house? I don't keep a gun."

Instantly I regretted adding the part about the gun, but my little-girl belief that all law enforcement officers could be trusted made me blurt it out before my grown-up cynicism could stop me. Now I watched the deputy for a sign of heightened interest in the remoteness of my situation, but there was none.

"You don't need a gun," he said. "I don't even let my girl-friend keep a gun. I gave her a can of Mace."

"I've already got one of those."

"Then I wouldn't worry," he said. "It's just kids."

"That seems to be the consensus," I said wryly. "Do you ever catch them?"

"Well, usually not."

"Don't they have anything else to do?"

"It's a game," he said.

"Some game. Theft. Vandalism. Destruction of federal property."

"That's why they like it, I guess. The risk."

I kicked at the gravel and thought about that. "Listen. You don't think—" I said. "I mean, surely it's not—"

The deputy glanced up from his writing.

"Could it be the neighbors?" I asked.

"Why would they do that?"

"You know. Getting even for last week. Like if they found out that I . . . you know."

He thought about it. "Well, maybe. It *is* a small town," he said. Then he added, "But I doubt it."

•

🏠 I learned later that Tony the mail carrier had picked up my bills; they'd still been in the mailbox when he made his rounds, even though it was on the ground. I brought up my tools and hammered out the dents and nailed it back on its post. It wobbled, but it held.

A few weeks later, the "kids" did score a home run. This time they also stole the mail: a letter and a picture of Max I was sending to Mom. This really made me mad. I imagined pimply teenage boys tearing open my letter and reading it, making crude jokes about it, then tossing it out the window, where it would lie on the road until passing traffic ground it into the dirt. I worried vaguely that they'd come steal Max or poison him or something.

A mile away at the low-water crossing, Skip found his mailbox in the creek.

That afternoon, I put my mailbox under the deck beside the lawn mower and rented a post office box, one of the few that were left, in town.

I also told everybody how mad I was. I told the lady at the checkout counter at the grocery store, the bank teller in Lawrence, and all my professors at the university. I e-mailed it to my computer pals and telephoned it to other people and wrote letters to my relatives. Some people I even told twice. Or tried to. "Listen. I am furious," I'd begin. "Have you ever heard of this baseball mailbox thing?"

"Is this about the kids who stole that picture of your dog?"

"Yeah—oh. I've already told you."

"Last week."

"Oh."

The more I told it, the madder I got. I started thinking about revenge. Never really intending to carry it through, still I fantasized. My favorite fantasy was Retribution by Shotgun. Years ago I'd given my shotgun away, but "if I still had my shotgun," I'd tell people, "you know what I'd do? I'd sit up there at night and wait for 'em to come back and then I'd blow holes in the side of their truck."

"That'd fix 'em up, all right," people would say, and I'd feel righteous. Never mind that my Sunday School teachers had etched the Golden Rule on the inside of my eyelids. Never mind that Jesus would have prayed over those kids, or Gandhi would have made friends with them, or the Buddha would have been laughing. My humanity was positively shellacking my divinity.

Several months later, a fellow named Jack came to stain the house. I liked Jack. He was a friendly, happy, generous man, and it tickled me to have him hanging around the study windows, singing to himself, while I worked. He and his wife were raising three daughters, he told me, and he was mostly concerned with teaching them to be good. "If they grow up to be good people, and care about people," he'd say, "that's all I could ask."

He must have been teaching by example, because one afternoon when I got home from school I found that he had discovered my beat-up mailbox, hammered it into shape, and nailed it back up. I'd never mentioned the vandalism to him; he'd simply seen a need and acted out of kindness. I was overcome. His thoughtfulness seemed to make up for that other reckless disregard.

I knew I should just thank him and leave things alone, but I didn't. Instead I thought: OPPORTUNITY.

Ignoring the certain knowledge that I was undoing all the good, the setting back to rights, the balancing that Jack had unknowingly accomplished, I sneaked down the driveway one afternoon when he was on the south side of the house and filled the mailbox full of rocks from the road. Then, keeping a nervous watch out for neighbors, I wrapped half a roll of glass tape around the mailbox and the arm of the post and twist-tied the mouth of the box shut with a piece of wire. Just let them slam into *that* with an aluminum bat, I thought.

As if that weren't bad enough, the next day, I confessed what I'd done to Jack, my innocent benefactor. My words tumbled out in a compulsive rush, and I couldn't get the slightest sense of what he was feeling. Surprise? Disappointment? Amusement? Whatever it was, he covered it with characteristic cheerfulness, saying that he couldn't blame me a bit for being mad and (chuckling) to be sure and let him know what happened.

That very night, late, I heard a truck pull up to the mailbox. I heard a gratifying *whannng!* and then: "OWWWW! What the *heck* is in there?"

I never could bring myself to tell Jack.

•

A man named Max Mountain once owned a hardware store down the road in Oskaloosa. An old fellow used to buy tools from the store—a pair of pliers, a screwdriver—take them home and use them, and then bring them back for a refund. He'd do this four or five times with the same tools. This finally made Max's clerk angry, and the clerk complained to Max about customers taking advantage of the store. Max shrugged. "They're just people," he said.

If you can't help someone, the Buddha said, then at least don't do things that cause harm.

But fear is a mind-killer. Fear takes away my power to reason and, as King Lear put it, that way madness lies. I become like a cavewoman, forgetting everything I think I know about humility and compassion, generosity and self-respect.

The mailbox is still on the post, still full of rocks. Every now and then I get the urge to take it down.

Digging Up Bones

*R*ight before Halloween I went to Kansas City for lunch with some friends and came home with a German shepherd puppy. On a whim, I'd found a breeder in the classifieds during dessert and decided to stop by on the way out of town. It's how I bought my Honda: turned in at the lot one day on the way home from school and traded in my overworked Metro. The Honda is green because it was the only one left.

On a whim is a fun way to live, because it's so spontaneous that by morning I've already forgotten what I did the day before. So when I look out the window and see that new car sitting in the driveway, or that big puppy flopping around in the yard, I get excited all over again. Whose car? I wonder. Where'd that dog come from? And then I realize.

The German shepherd puppy was eleven weeks old when I brought him home to meet Max, but he already weighed twice that many pounds. His feet were the size of dinner plates. In the sun, his eyes were gold. I named him Red.

Red was a fat, furry, constantly moving ball of doggy energy. I'd had a German shepherd before, but she liked to lie around in the air-conditioning and hide under the bed when company came. Red preferred to run, bite, sniff, leap, lick, and chase the stick. Max, being a serious, contemplative dog, didn't like him at first. When he saw Red gallumphing toward him in a joyful frenzy, he climbed into his doghouse and sat across the entrance. When Max went out on patrols, he made Red stay home.

I used to worry about Red because he was so reckless and uncoordinated. He knew how to go fast but he hadn't figured out how to stop, and he was always tripping over his feet and tumbling headlong down the kitchen steps.

On warm days I kept the sliding glass door open but closed the screen, to keep the dogs out of the house. One morning I was in the den, sweeping, when I heard a loud *flumph!* outside. I rushed onto the deck and found Red splayed on the ground ten feet below like a flattened Wile E. Coyote in a Road Runner cartoon. "Oh, no! Red!" I shouted, and ran down to see if he was dead. When I reached him he gave me a dazed look, shook his head, then struggled to his feet and gallumphed away.

Red is not a show-quality dog because his eyes bug out like Ping-Pong balls. Sometimes when he gets excited I worry that they're going to pop right out of his head and I won't be able to put them back.

Red has some kind of sleep apnea, because he holds his breath in his sleep. I had a husband with sleep apnea once, but never a dog. I also never had a dog who snores.

Max doesn't snore, but he coughs like a chicken bone is stuck in his throat. He eats cicadas like popcorn and the only thing that scares him is thunder. He doesn't care for brooms. If I light a match, he goes somewhere else. Like a cat, he hides bites of dogfood in the folds of the bedspread.

Red carries his supper all over the house, leaving trails of it behind so he can track it down later.

Red likes to plop his big feet down in the water bowl. He likes to put his whole head into the bucket under the spigot and then bring his dripping muzzle across the yard and lay it in your lap, or nuzzle your bare leg with it. When I go jogging down the driveway, he charges into the pond like a surfer at a beach party. When it rains, he sits unsheltered in the yard and blinks at the drops that fall on his face.

Max prefers not to be wet at any time. If he goes to the pond for a drink, he stands at the bare edge in a backward slant and stretches his neck way out so that his tongue barely touches the surface of the water. If a wavelet threatens to dampen his paws, he leaps away like a skittish colt. If he feels a drop of rain, he goes into his doghouse.

The dogs like to leave little presents for me in the house. One day I came home after school and was putting away some of my clutter before I let them in for the night. Noticing a pile of socks on the bed, I grabbed them, and then I screamed. They weren't socks. They were a thrown-up squirrel.

Another time I looked out the window and saw Red with a pelvic bone in his mouth, to which two long leg bones were attached. I'm sure they were only deer bones, but it did give me a start, the way they dangled down to those big foot bones. It occurred to me to call the sheriff, but I didn't. I've always loved a mystery. I once had an Italian boyfriend with ties to the underworld, and that was like living in a Mario Puzo novel. But when his friends stole my silver, tapped my phone, and introduced me to a state representative who wanted a massage, I decided it was time to move on.

🏠 Halfway into my first semester at K. U., I was coming home late from a night class when I noticed behind me, as I drove through north Lawrence, an older-model pickup truck with one headlight. The driver was a big man with unruly hair: I could see his silhouette as we sat at a traffic light. I changed lanes a few times, but the pickup stayed back there.

When I reached the first turn several miles from town, I considered going straight. But I turned toward home anyway, thinking the truck might not really be following me; it might only be going in my direction. Lots of people lived down this road. But the truck turned, too.

I jammed down the accelerator, to see if the truck would

keep up. It did. I slowed to a crawl, thinking it would pass me. It didn't.

For the moment, my car phone was useless: I was too far from a tower.

Eight miles later, I came to the dirt road that led home. This time, I didn't turn. If the pickup *was* following me, I wasn't about to lead the man straight to where I lived. Instead, I raced to a fork. One road took me up the hill to McLouth; maybe the pickup would go the other way, toward Oskaloosa.

On the other hand, I thought, maybe the man lived around here. Many people commuted to Lawrence—although probably not at midnight.

When I looked back, the pickup was coming around the fork, too.

In McLouth I turned onto a residential street and sped by the houses, but before long I saw the pickup barreling down a hill behind me. I turned a corner and raced to the end of the block, where I stopped beside the post office. If the pickup wasn't following me, I'd be able to see it go by on the main road.

Seconds passed, but the truck didn't appear.

Then, in my rearview mirror, I glimpsed it edging around the corner.

Now I was scared. This place, like every place, has its demons. One man down the road strangled his wife and put her down a well. Not far away, a woman and her lover shot the woman's boyfriend and sank him in her uncle's pond.

It had struck me some time back, during the few minutes I'd been within range of a cell tower, that I could simply pick up the car phone and call the sheriff. But I kept thinking that my mystery-loving imagination was working overtime, that the truck was like the one-armed man in *The Fugitive* and its missing headlight made it seem more threatening than it really was.

Besides, I was embarrassed about the times I'd already called—once about my neighbors, twice about a smashed mailbox. But now, with that single headlight glaring through my back window and an escaped axe murderer, for all I knew, behind the wheel, I'd gladly have called in a whole regiment of sheriffs if they could have saved me.

I tore around the corner, doubled back to the main road, and went back the way I'd come, thinking that if the pickup was still following me when I got to the fork, I'd go to some stranger's house and ask for help. By the time I got to the turn, I couldn't see the truck. When I reached the dirt road home, the truck was gone.

I fled over those three miles of gravel road like a banshee, raced down the driveway, ran into the house with the dogs, and locked the door. As soon as I knew I was safe, I burst into tears.

Finally, I called the sheriff.

"I didn't want to cry wolf," I explained, now realizing how foolish that sounded.

The deputy was insistent. "You should call us even if you only suspect trouble," he said. "We can send someone to meet you."

"But it seemed so unimportant," I said, "compared to the other things you have to do."

"Ma'am," he said with an edge of impatience, "it's what we're here for."

I filed the report, but I couldn't remember which headlight was out.

Pretty Boy Floyd

$\mathcal{W}$hen he showed up in the yard in the dead of winter
he was scrawny and hungry and he wouldn't let me touch
him, even though he had those soulful brown eyes that
made him look like he'd already forgiven the world for all its
meanness.

I kept calling him Pretty Boy, so in time it naturally came
out that his name was Floyd. Part husky and part something
else, like keeshond or maybe chow, he had a white blaze
down his nose and white feet and a thick coat of dirty matted fur that badly needed a good shampoo and conditioning
rinse.

He also needed a trip to the vet and shots. I thought
about not keeping him at first, because a third dog just
seemed like one too many, no matter how much he needed
somebody (me) to care for him. Besides, who could provide

for three dogs on a graduate student's stipend and still have money left over for pizza?

But after he'd been hanging around a few weeks, one day after a short display of putting up resistance, cringing and backing away and rolling his eyes, he let me catch him. I was so flattered that I decided to resign myself to beans and rice or something equally cost-effective so I could keep feeding him. I remembered that my third ex-husband Terry had lived on popcorn once.

When I took Floyd to the vet, the main thing wrong with him was that he was starving, even though he'd been eating at the house of steps for a month. Fifteen pounds under-weight, he was lighter than Max, although he stood six inches taller. The rest of the day we spent at the Doggie Mat, where I washed him and untangled the burrs from his coat. He turned out a golden-haired, good-humored dog with limitless energy who loves to howl.

Floyd howls for absolutely no reason and at any time of the day. Sometimes when I talk to him, he howls at me and leaps around in a happy frenzy. This gets Red going and then there's a duet, and if I add my voice we have a trio: Floyd as soprano, me as alto, Red as tenor. Max sits and watches, cocking his straight-up ear. Max never howls.

I once found a skinny flea-covered bird dog digging in a dumpster on the side of the road, but I couldn't take him. I had enough dogs already.

I found a tough little terrier roaming the downtown streets near a catfish restaurant. I gave him to the dispatcher at the police station on the way home.

I also found a badly wounded beagle lying in the highway, having been hit by a car or perhaps, the vet said, deliberately thrown out. We put him to sleep.

I found a Himalayan cat once whose pink sore-covered skin showed through in great patches where her fur had matted and pulled away from her body. I left her at the pound, but ended up taking her back when no one wanted her. I had her shaved and given shots and treated for fleas, and before I knew it she was a luxurious snow-white beauty. A few months later a woman who had always wanted a Himalayan took her in.

I have a hard time making these decisions, whether to leave strays where I find them or take them home to my house, give them up to the pound, or find someone else who wants them. I suppose they cross my path because I have this dilemma.

I was standing outside a Wal-Mart once when I noticed a car that didn't move when the traffic light turned green. Traffic behind it piled up, and people blew horns. Still the car didn't move. It occurred to me that the driver was in some kind of trouble, and I thought of going back inside and getting help. But I didn't. I went on to my car and started home. As I pulled out of the parking lot, I saw an ambulance coming. Later I learned that the woman driving the stopped car was having a stroke.

The other day in the grocery store parking lot I walked right into the middle of a screaming fight between a big blond woman and a thin dark-haired woman who was holding a little boy by the hand. They were so excited I couldn't understand what they were yelling about, until finally the blond woman turned to go back in the store and muttered something about the dark-haired woman hitting the child for no good reason.

I've seen women in the laundromat slapping their children around, but I've never said anything. Once when I was putting my clothes back in the car, I noticed a stooped old man in an ill-fitting blazer trudging through the parking lot toward a woman who was standing in front of a neighborhood bar. The back of the old man's pants was streaked with brown, and his movements seemed painful. He walked with a cane. As soon as the woman saw him, she started shouting at him, though he was still thirty paces away. "Baaah!" she screamed. "We had a date thirty minutes ago but you're LATE so I'm LEAVING! I can't wait for you forever, Billy!" She got into a van and drove away. Gasping from the effort of walking, Billy stopped where he was and leaned against a truck. He watched until the van was out of sight, then shook his head and shuffled to the bar.

Robert Pogue Harrison has written that all we have to learn about what is real and not-real lies in the exteriority of our inner lives. But when people's inner lives flash in front of me like that, right in the middle of a suburban parking lot, I feel like a squirrel caught treading on a limb too thin, and if I step forward into the fray the limb will break; but it's just as fragile where I'm standing.

Mouse Tales

Nothing happens in contradiction to nature,
only in contradiction to what we know of it.

> Agent Dana Scully,
> *X-Files*

I can tell how big the mice are in my house by the kind of evidence they leave behind. Usually it's small and comes in bunches, and if I pay attention I can see what they've been eating that belongs to me. When they've been eating the dishwashing sponge, the evidence is pink or yellow or green. When they've been eating the wooden spoons, the evidence has splinters. When they can't find anything to eat, they don't leave much evidence.

One mouse that left big lumps of multicolored evidence all over the kitchen turned out to be a squirrel. He ran up and down inside the walls at night, chattering at all hours. He once ate a whole bag of Ruffles potato chips. He left behind a shiny trail of foil bits that led from the pantry shelf across the kitchen floor to the top of the microwave and disappeared into a hole behind the refrigerator.

So squirrels like potato chips. And mice are nuts about chocolate.

I discovered that mice like chocolate the night I heard them moving the cans around on the pantry shelves and the next morning I found a box of Hershey's cocoa pushed over on its side. A team of craven mice had tried to gnaw through the plastic top: they had left tiny teeth marks all the way around the edge. Soon after that, they ate half a pan of brownies I'd left out on the kitchen counter. Then they got into the miniature Three Musketeers bars and ate those up. When I went looking for my Hershey's Nuggets, those delicious individually wrapped blocks of chocolate with almonds that I was keeping in a bowl on the shelf over the stove, I found only the empty bag, along with some telltale holes in the plastic.

But that's nothing compared to when the mouse got into the tea pitcher.

Before I went to bed one night I washed my plastic iced-tea pitcher, dried it, and left it on the counter by the sink. The pitcher doesn't weigh more than a few ounces and stands twelve inches tall. Next day, I made a pot of tea, but when I picked up the empty pitcher to pour in the tea, I heard a faint rattle in the bottom. I turned it upside down and out fell . . . mouse evidence. It dropped into the sink with a *clink!*

I have always heard that a mouse will hop. Although I've never seen one, a hopping mouse is something I can picture. To get to the fourth pantry shelf from the bottom, where I used to keep the cocoa, a mouse might have to do some insignificant hopping.

But what I can't picture is how a mouse the size of the one that left the evidence in the bottom of my tea pitcher can leap straight up, twelve inches into the air, like Magic Johnson, and land sturdily in the bottom of a tall, empty, practically weightless tea pitcher without knocking it over, and scratch around in the bottom for a while, until he finds out there's nothing in it he's interested in, whereupon he'd leave some little calling cards, to let me know he stopped by—and then hop out, twelve inches straight up again, and land feet-first on the counter, and then continue his nightly rounds, maybe dropping by the stove on his way out to see if I had left any spilled spaghetti sauce, and then saunter away into the night, as if absolutely nothing . . .

extraordinary . . .

had happened.

Magic

God is alive; magic is afoot.

Buffy Sainte-Marie

$\mathcal{A}$t the Red Earth powwow in Oklahoma City I bought a pair of beaded earrings that were prettier than any I'd ever seen. I couldn't take my eyes off them. I wish I knew the artisan's name who made them, but I don't. It embarrasses me to admit that. It's like when people say, Oh, I just *adored* such-and-such a book, you've *got* to read it, and I say, Who's the author? and they say, I can't remember the author's name.

Anyway, I was short of cash, so my friend Frank loaned me the forty dollars to buy those earrings, long crystal cylinders with pale pink and blue beads at the bottom. They didn't quite brush the tops of my shoulders. They tinkled faintly beside my ear, like tiny wind chimes, and the sound could take me out of time. I'd be walking up the stairs to my old office in Overland Park and hear that sound and suddenly

I'd be standing in a Kansas field, feeling the breeze on my face.

Once I handed those earrings to a woman in a bar who admired them. She put them on and looked at herself in a mirror, and she was so taken with them that I gave them to her. Soon afterword, I dreamed about them. I was standing at a window in a tall house, looking out on a flat, colorless landscape. In the distance I could see the earrings, transformed into a crystal castle, suspended and shimmering like clear birds in the sky, surrounded by light. I was struck with wonder, and I awoke with a sense of longing, like a lost child on an unfamiliar path who knows that home is behind the mountain but doesn't know how to get there.

That was ten years ago. This summer, I came across something St. Teresa of Ávila wrote, in a book called *The Interior Castle*. "Our soul is like a castle made of a diamond or clear crystal," she wrote, "in which there are many rooms."

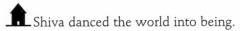 Shiva danced the world into being.

At an art fair in Olathe, Kansas, I saw an artist drawing portraits. Beside him was a cardboard box of faces he had drawn at different times, and I started flipping through them, struck by the artist's sensitive hand. I found the profile of an African boy maybe two years old. He wore delicate yellow beads, and his shoulders were too thin. The piece was done in charcoal, and the eyes held a quality of sadness, of sorrow that seemed far older than the child.

"Who is this?" I asked the artist, whose name was Ray

Craighead. He was sketching a teenage girl who sat uncomfortably in a straight chair nearby.

He glanced at the drawing. "Oh, no one in particular," he said. "I support the world's effort to feed starving children, and he just came into my head and I drew him."

Ray Craighead danced that child into being.

"How much do you want for it?" I asked.

"Twenty-five dollars?"

I looked in my wallet. "I've got twenty."

He shrugged. "Okay."

I handed him the drawing to sign because he had forgotten. Now it hangs over my printer. Last week my friend Beth saw it for the first time. I went downstairs to make tea and when I came back she was standing before the portrait with tears in her eyes. "Someone took great care here," she said.

▲ Wonder, wrote Thomas Carlyle, is the basis of worship.

In front of my monitor are four carved Masai elders in red robes, squatting around a cup of water, that I bought from a Savannah dealer in African art when I lived at the cabin. I'd had to ask Mom for gas money for that trip to Savannah to visit my sister Kelly, but when I saw those Masai elders I just handed over my credit card. Now when I come into the study to write, I fancy that in the night, while I was sleeping, they've moved.

I found a carved Honduran box at a Mennonite gift shop outside Americus, Georgia, one summer day when MaRe and I had lunch at their restaurant. The carving, which covered most of the large box, was of a tropical town with whitewashed houses and thatched roofs. A woman walks away down a road, holding a basket on her head. The scene seemed so real, it drew me in. I couldn't afford to buy the box, but I couldn't stay away from it, either. I kept going back to look at it. Three months later MaRe and I went to the restaurant again. The Honduran box was still in the shop. Ignoring that I'd been trying to pay off that credit card for months, I charged the box. Now it holds my Christmas decorations. Every time I dust it, I'm in Honduras.

Suzuki said that ordinary life itself is enlightenment. Maybe ordinary things are, too. They touch something inside me, something that feels emotions I don't have a name for.

Land can do that to me. Some places, like the Georgia pond where I used to live, or the Florida Gulf on a still day, or eighty acres in Kansas that I almost bought once, they move me, move inside me somehow. Going there is like stepping into a cathedral. A calmness takes me. Standing in a brome field beside a draw, examining a jade-colored stone worn smooth by water, I hear a solitary meadowlark calling from a fence post, and suddenly I absorb the place like sunlight. I don't think about it so much as that it's just in me, a clear space I can go back to and rest in on days when I can't put my feet on that ground. Whatever I do, wherever I go, the spirit of the place stays with me, quieting me, like an arm of the Great Comforter, in an embrace that enfolds completely.

It seems strange to me that the material world can soothe so deeply: that's a virtue I've always reserved to God. But because I can't touch the face of God I guess I find the Honduran box, and the Masai elders, and the artist's dream of a starving child that I think I sense God in and hold them close to me. It's like leaving the light on in the house when I go out for a walk. Coming back in the dark, I see that light in the distance and it's warm and beckoning, a consolatory refuge at the center of my troubled uncertainty. I surround myself with the things that reach the place in me that loves, that is open, that knows beauty and joy and wonder, and remember that the whole world is God, if I will only open my eyes.

"Let's see if I've got this right," she would say to herself. "I've taken an inert gas that's in the air, made it into a liquid, put some impurities into a ruby, attached a magnet, and detected the fires of creation."

Ellie, from *Contact*
by Carl Sagan

The Girl Who Could Talk to Trees

*I*n the beginning was the land, wrote Ferrol Sams.

Then came trees.

Seventy miles south of Kansas City and a half-mile hike over grazing land lie eighty acres of tree-covered bluffs, two pastures, a field of soybeans, and part of a rocky creek I almost bought once. I called the place Many Paths because of a maze of overgrown roads and animal trails that wove through the woods and down to the water.

In a large clearing on a west-facing bluff high above the creek stood a cottonwood with a broken limb, which marked a place where I liked to camp. I called the place Broken Branch. I spent summer weekends there with a borrowed family-size tent, a cooler full of food, and a book. In the late afternoon I stretched my tarp between tree trunks, hung my lantern from a branch, built my campfire with sticks, and sat on a log.

I didn't know the names then, but I can call them now: hickory, oak, black walnut, ash, maple, locust, basswood, sycamore, cottonwood. There were thousands. There were so many that, when I went to Many Paths, what most claimed my attention was not bluffs nor rocks nor creek nor trails, but trees. They had a distinct presence, a kind of collective benevolence, that never altered with the weather or the season. They talked ceaselessly. "Shhhhhh," they'd say, or "SHHHHH," their leaves rustling, rustling in the wind. Like Tolkien's tree-people, the Ents, they seemed to be hiding an enormous well beneath them, filled up with ages of memory and long, slow, steady thinking, while their surfaces sparkled with the present.

When she was a girl, an Oklahoma woman I know was best friends with an old sycamore in her back pasture. She ran to it when she was hurt or sad and sat under it and cried and told it her troubles, and it sang to her and told her its secrets.

"What kind of secrets?" I asked.

She couldn't remember. "Trees have their own language," she said, "but I've forgotten it now."

I never thought to question whether her story was true. It only made me wonder what great stories I'd been missing. I wonder if I'm still young enough to hear them.

La Belle Dame sans Regrets

Je ne comprends pas bien
La Belle Dame sans Regrets.

Sting

*U*nless you count the fold-out rose on the Hallmark card from my mother or the rose-bordered e-mailed greetings from friends, not a single flower graced my doorstep on Valentine's Day. No armfuls of red roses borne by harried florists, no heart-shaped boxes of chocolates wrapped in red cellophane, not even a grandmotherly arrangement of red carnations found me out.

I'm remembering the year I was twelve, when Gary Paulk brought me a dozen red roses in a milk-glass vase and one of those giant heart-shaped boxes of chocolates with the plastic flowers on top, which embarrassed me after I thought about it, since everybody knows the size of the heart tells how much a person likes you and I knew the candy had come from the drugstore downtown. In a place the size of

Ocilla, Georgia, where I grew up, word gets around. And it's a fact that at choir practice on Wednesday night several people winked at me.

Along with the roses and the candy Gary Paulk also gave me a pink stuffed pig, in remembrance of the pigs he was raising on his daddy's farm. I named the pig Hugo, after Gary Paulk's middle name, which Mom and I secretly pronounced Hug-o. Unlike Gary Paulk's pigs, Hug-o reeked with Gary Paulk's British Sterling after-shave, so I didn't stop sleeping with Hug-o until Gary Paulk and I broke up. Because even at twelve, some things you have ideas about. Especially if you read a lot, and MaRe was always leaving these racy historical romances lying around.

Gary Paulk was the first great romance in my lifelong saga of great romances, where all the boys played heroes while I was the *femme fatale*. Or rather *la belle dame sans merci*. Some of my heroes are still in recovery.

How my romance started with Gary Paulk was, even though I was wearing braces and ugly black-rimmed glasses at the time, I and most of the other girls in my class had a heart-stopping crush on him. He was handsome and smart and athletic and older. I thought I'd die from that crush, it was so painful. I used to stand in front of my bedroom window and dance to Elvis Presley singing "You Don't Know Me" and watch the cars go by, imagining that every one of them was Miss Judy taking Gary Paulk home from tennis practice. The Paulks were country folks, with a big farmhouse and a cabin on a lake, and peanut fields and pigs, and Gary Paulk had a motorcycle and a ski boat and a good-looking cousin named Howard with a fast car, and that was all very wild and exciting to a town girl like me.

Gary Paulk and I got to know each other when I was eleven, when Mr. Sconyers took us on a field trip to St. Augustine. Somehow Gary Paulk and I got squeezed side by side into the back seat of Mr. Sconyers's car, even though Gary Paulk was supposed to be going with Joy Jeffries at the time. I don't know where Joy was that day. I don't know where anybody was except Gary Paulk. All I remember is what I was wearing, which was yellow culottes and a sleeveless floral print blouse, and hardly being able to breathe from getting to touch Gary Paulk's arm all the way to Florida.

In St. Augustine we visited the wax museum, the Ripley's Believe-It-Or-Not Museum, the Old Spanish Fort, and the Fountain of Youth, and I have a vague recollection of some of the boys putting firecrackers in people's Cokes at the Dairy Queen. But what I noticed most was the side of Gary Paulk's head and how his brown hair came down over the top of his ear, and him laughing. Gary Paulk always did laugh a lot. It was one of the things I liked about him.

By the time we got to Marine Land the day was almost over. The thought of wrenching myself away from the tall, good-natured boy by my side was dragging at me like an anchor, weighing down my aching heart, when right there before God and everybody, in front of the aquarium on the way down to the amphitheater, where the dolphins were swimming in a turquoise pool, Gary Paulk grabbed my hand and didn't let go. After that, all I knew was that somewhere between Marine Land and Ocilla the sun went down.

Nevertheless, Gary Paulk and I didn't start going together until Mr. Sconyers started the ballroom dancing class.

The ballroom dancing class was where Mr. Sconyers taught us to waltz and foxtrot in the lunchroom during sixth period. Some of the older kids were in that class, including Gary Paulk, and sometimes Gary Paulk and I danced together. We were especially good at the cha-cha-cha. One day, Gary Paulk dropped something into the pocket of my denim smock as he blew by me on his way out of the lunchroom after class. It was his I.D. bracelet, which Joy Jeffries was reported to have given him as a present, and a question he had scribbled on a scrap of notebook paper.

"Will you go with me?" the note said.

I went weak at the knees, after which I screamed. Diane Norton said he was just trying to make Joy Jeffries jealous, but I didn't believe it because of St. Augustine. Gary Paulk and I never talked about St. Augustine after we got back, but some things a girl just knows.

My relationship with Gary Paulk turned into a long adolescent romance that was helped along by British Sterling, "We've Only Just Begun" by the Carpenters, motorcycle rides in the country, rainy evenings in Gary Paulk's porch swing, fishing, slow-dancing, and late-night telephone conversations made up of sweet talk and breathless silences that seemed to stretch out forever into small, quilted infinities of comfort. For more than two years, I was caught up in all that soft pink easiness, held close in Gary Paulk's warmhearted dependability and his solid values and his family who, like him, laughed all the time and who still, years after I'd left home and many of the parents I'd known, including mine, had divorced, hung together through the arduous but carefully watched, well-supported procession into adulthood and changing fortunes of the four Paulk sons.

But then I turned thirteen. I left for summer school in North Carolina clutching dear old Hug-o to my breast and carrying a sack full of love letters on cassette tapes that Gary Paulk had tearfully recorded in the weeks before I went away. Halfway through the summer I stopped listening. I came back to Georgia in August having left my small-town past disdainfully behind. I'd seen a bigger world in North Carolina, learned some new music. No more Carpenters for me. No more Mamas and Papas. I wanted Neil Young. Bob Dylan. The Beatles. I'd met a boy named Alan in North Carolina, and he'd taught me some hard facts to attach to my airy romance-novel ideas. So without even a hint of sympathy, without the slimmest regret, I dumped the faithful Gary Paulk the day he came to welcome me home. I couldn't get rid of him fast enough. *La belle dame sans merci.* I thought I'd outgrown him.

Now Gary Paulk has a daughter named Amy and three other children, and he lives with his wife of many years on the old farm near his folks. He tends a vineyard, and I expect he makes wine. Sometimes when I go back home I see him, taking his boys to the show or his family to supper. They're a laughing, comfortable knot of a family, and they belong in that place where the nights are warm and the summers are

long, where the fishing is good and the pastel sky deepens
into rose at sunset.

As for me, husbands came and husbands went, and
so did some other men. There was the poet-politician. The
dentist-perfectionist. The car salesman who liked to read.
The alcoholic comedian. The pilot-adventurer. The brilliant
entrepreneur. The cowboy who lied but looked fine in his
Wranglers. Some of them could dance, but they were never
the ones I expected. We threaded through each other's lives
but the knots never held: I was always declaring indepen-
dence, unraveling the weave.

Before winter set in at the house of steps, I was wan-
dering around outside, picking up the sticks that the dogs
had strewn around the yard and tossing them back into the
woods. It was October, windy and gray and cold. The trees
were bare. Snow was coming.

I went into the sauna to check on the dogs' food because
the cardinals had been stealing it. They'd perch on the edge
of the bowl, pick out a lump, and fly away. I was filling the
bowl when I heard a faint thumping at one of the windows.
Thinking it was a hedge-apple branch being knocked around
by the wind, I didn't bother to look, and I finished with the
dog food and was about to go out again when I noticed a
movement on the windowsill, which forms a wide inset
ledge along the wall. A tufted titmouse had flown in through
the open door and was trotting back and forth, back and
forth, along the sill. Occasionally, he lunged toward the sky

behind the windowpane. Every time he lunged, he thumped against the glass.

I covered my hand with the end of the frayed flannel shirt I was wearing and caught him, trying not to squeeze him too hard, and took him out to the porch. I rubbed his head once with my finger and let him go. He flew west, with a bit of thread from my sleeve caught on his claw. I keep birdseed in the feeder, but I don't know whether he's been back.

Things I Like About Living Alone

I'm sitting at the chapel window in the late afternoon on the Sunday after Valentine's Day, still wearing the blue long johns and flowered flannel pajama top I slept in. I did trade in my red slippers for my Nikes a few hours ago because I had to check on the dog food outside, but my hair's a mess and the cereal bowl is still in the sink from breakfast and there's a pot of chili cooling on the stove from supper, which I ate with raw onion an hour ago.

Here's where I keep the coffeepot: beside the bed. It seems like a contradiction to have it anywhere else. If I have to get up in the morning, I can set the timer and wake up to the sound of freshly brewed Colombian Supremo trickling into the pot. If I don't have to get up, I can roll over whenever I feel like it and flip the switch, and a few minutes later the aroma of steaming coffee is wafting through the room and I'm sitting with my back against the pillows, drinking from my Earth Mother mug and looking out the window at the sunlight breaking through the hickories.

Sometimes, if I have them, I put powdered-sugar doughnuts beside the coffeepot. But Rice Krispies squares are the best.

Here's what I do at night to make myself sleepy: play Scrabble in bed. If I'm not in the mood for Scrabble, I do crossword puzzles.

Sometimes I like to make my supper out of all one thing, like all rice. Or all Green Giant handpicked asparagus. Or all pancakes or salad or black beans.

If I have leftovers, I can put them together and make combo suppers, like pancakes and beans, or salad with rice and asparagus.

If I feel like it, I can have lunch for breakfast and breakfast for lunch. When I have bagels, I lick the cream cheese off the knife.

Sometimes I'm not a vegetarian.

Sometimes I write and sometimes I read and sometimes I work on my Welsh castle jigsaw puzzle all day long: it's three thousand pieces.

In December, I sat in the bed for two days and folded origami Christmas presents, multicolored ducks and rockets and boats and little nuns.

Sometimes I wear my clothes inside out.

I can go all day without uttering a sound unless the phone rings, and sometimes I unplug it.

I let Max sleep on the furniture.

I've been thinking about adopting a cat.

One day I surprised myself and brought home a new sofa.

I don't always put the top back on the toothpaste and sometimes I leave my clothes on the floor. I never close the bathroom door except in winter, and I never go to the laundromat until I run out of clean underwear. If I'm not in the mood, I don't make the bed. Sometimes I wear my pajamas all day long. I watch television whenever I feel like it and turn the stereo up loud in the middle of the night. I've seen *Becket* seventeen times. I can work out at midnight or go to bed at nine. If I go into town, I don't have to say when I'll be back.

But mostly it's the quiet I like best about living alone, a quality of silence that even in the most companionable company is not the same when company's around. Sometimes, it's the quiet of sounds.

The Georgia cabin I lived in sat directly under the flight path for a fighter wing from Moody Air Force Base in Valdosta. The fighters screamed over at treetop level, which drove the cats under the bed. When I went walking with the dogs, I stood in the field and watched the silent planes fight mock battles high in the air, climbing and dropping around each other in elliptical patterns, leaving behind white bursts of trail, like Japanese calligraphy in the sky. When the base helicopters flew over the pond, the rhythm of their propellers started all the big frogs singing.

Most of the year, the hum of farm machinery drifted down to the cabin. Tractors cultivated, seeded, fertilized, and plowed. Irrigation pumps droned night and day. Combines shucked and shelled, balers baled, crop dusters dipped and sprayed. Into the brief moments between the stopping of one engine and the starting of another, the cacophony of pond voices burst like a piñata spilling candy over children. They were the voices of bullfrog, tree frog, crow, and blackbird, bobwhite and hawk and cicada, mourning dove and cricket—or at evening, barred owl, whippoorwill, coyote. When my cousins came night fishing, the echo of their laughter, the plop of a lure landing in the shallows, the scrape of a paddle against the side of the boat carried over the water to where I sat on the back steps, listening.

Fall brought the profoundest quiet, when a light rain would continue for days, coming straight down, because not even the slightest breeze disturbed the air. I'd leave the cabin door open and sit in the den with a book, and except for the turning of pages I'd keep silent company with the constant patter, patter, patter of the rain on the leaves, the low songs of the bullfrogs, the splash of a young bass after a fly, the notes of a solitary robin.

In my northeastern Kansas yard, a bird feeder so tall I have to climb a ladder to fill it is a gathering place for woodpeckers, goldfinches, cardinals, and chickadees. All day long as I listen from the den window, the birds chatter and peep and chirp, coming and going in quick, noisy processions, taking the seed away little by little, like small waves that burst onto a beach and carry grains of sand back to the sea. At evening, mourning doves call, and tree frogs and crickets chirp. At bedtime the uncivilized owls cackle and howl in the woods behind the house; and the whippoorwills, too loud near the windows, and a cricket on the brick floor in the kitchen keep me awake. Sometimes, the south wind brings the sound of a train clacking through the river valley ten miles away. My dogs bark at an old hound baying up the hill.

Even in the country, there is rarely any pure silence. Sound is omnipresent, and it moves through my minutes and days and years like breathing. Unseen, even unnoticed, like the rustle of dry grass on a prairie, sound is a continuous undercurrent, drifting from bird to dog to train to myself and back to bird again. The essence of life distilled in life's utterings, sound seems, as Thoreau wrote, the very grain and stuff of which eternity is made. Sound unifies all things and is never still.

But sometimes in Kansas, around the house of steps, the quiet empties. In winter, with the land covered in snow, I sit on the deck late at night and listen. After a long time, a truck might go by on the road, or a cow in some farmer's field might low in distress, or a dog might bark or a tree branch break or a coyote howl, but these sounds are not constants. They are random and infrequent, like deer coming to drink from a creek.

Last night I was standing in the yard with the dogs, watching a comet in the northwest sky. It traveled faster than I could imagine, but even with my field glasses the only evidence of its movement that I could see was the luminous tail it left behind.

Down below, where the dogs and I shuffled around, the rustle of our footsteps unraveled the quiet, while in the vacuum of black space a mass of concentrated energy burned in utter silence.

Cultivate the silence, Joe told me once. It's the place from which renewal comes.

Alone in my hermit's life in Georgia I knew an old, mossy, pine-scented silence; now I'm coming to know this vast midwestern soundlessness. It's not a dark silence, like the one that creeps down the back of my neck when I jerk awake in the middle of the night, but a vibrant silence, a kind of earnest quietness, like an empty cup held out, a curtain about to rise, an owl in flight toward its nest. It's hidden on my walks, in my work, and in my sleep, waiting like a farm at the beginning of the day.

Birthday Revue

There will always by something to believe in.

Shawn Colvin,
"Steady On"

Today I'm thirty-nine.

The fun thing about living by myself a thousand miles from home is that sometimes all the birthday cards come early. My relatives must have been on the lookout for March this year, because I've been getting cards since the end of February. Which is exciting, because it stretches my birthday out. I don't wake up one morning and say, Oh, goody, today's my birthday—and then the next morning get up and remember it's over. It keeps going.

Some of the birthday cards came with checks. That's always nice. Sometimes it's even a relief, especially when I'm wondering how I'm going to pay the accountant. But this is an advantage to having a birthday at the end of March: I can pay the accountant with my birthday money. Then if I'm not happy with my taxes, I can make him feel guilty. "Hey,

Mike. This is my birthday money I'm paying you with," I can tell him.

"Gee, that's too bad," he'll say. "But—"

"I was going to adopt a blind starving child in Guatemala, Mike," I can say. "But [sigh] I'm paying you instead."

Another interesting thing about living alone is that if I feel like hearing the birthday song, I have to sing it to myself. This morning I drank my coffee, let the dogs out, and ate a bowl of Life cereal before I remembered it was my birthday, and then I sat on the edge of the bed with my coffee mug and sang happy birthday to Amy Blackmarr. It reminded me of when I was three, and I was standing on a chair in front of my birthday cake, which looked like a carousel. It had horses and played music. I wanted my party to begin, so I sang the birthday song to myself really loud. When my family heard me, they came in and started the party.

If I had to choose my favorite birthday, it would probably be the one where I turned ten and Sherry Cumby fainted.

Sherry Cumby was my next-door neighbor until I was eight. She was a sweet child with a cheerful disposition, big brown eyes, and long brown hair. What I liked about her was that she could always come out and play, and we hardly ever had a fight except when she spent the night at my house and we slept feet-to-feet on the den sofa with our feet touching.

The year I turned ten, Mom held my birthday party at my piano teacher's farmhouse in the country. MaRe had to bake two birthday cakes because we'd invited so many children.

The party started in the afternoon and lasted until after supper, because we were having a cookout. I had also planned a séance for around sunset, along with a surprise that Daddy and I had cooked up.

When the time came for the séance, all the children gathered around a big table on the screened porch. I was the spiritual medium, and I made everybody hold hands. "We have to make an unbroken circle or the ghost won't come," I explained to the boys, who were protesting.

I was very serious. I put a lighted candle in the middle of the table and started calling spirits, including the ghost of Benjamin Franklin. (We always called on the ghost of Benjamin Franklin at séances. Who knows why.) Mom and Miss Betty stood in the doorway, watching.

Then all of a sudden, the table hopped! Something knocked on it twice! Bill Rutherford shouted that an invisible person was kicking him. Somebody yelled. I closed my eyes and chanted, "If you goooo into the bathroom, and looook out the window, the ghoooost of Old Man Haaaarper will appear!"

Everybody raced to the bathroom. The window was behind the toilet. My friends clambered over each other, all trying to see outside at once. Presently, a white form appeared at the corner of the barn. "There he is!" I shouted. "There's Old Man Harper! Aaaagh!"

The ghost booed and gyrated and carried on, and when the kids in front had stared long enough for the idea to sink in, they tore out of the bathroom screaming. Then the second wave of kids ran out screaming. Then poor old Sherry Cumby, she took one look at that apparition flailing in the barnyard and fainted into a dead heap right there on top of the john. It took a confession from my dad, the production of the ghost-sheet, and the devouring of both birthday cakes and all the little cardboard cartons of vanilla ice cream before we settled down again. I sent everybody home with party favors of wax lips and plastic pumpkins full of candy corn left over from Halloween.

I remember another birthday party, this one at the cabin, when Charles Gibson brought a squirrel monkey, which he carried around on his shoulder and which bit everybody, including Charles Gibson. He also brought a shoe box in which he was raising a baby alligator he'd found in the ditch by his house. He wanted to let it loose in the pond. Maybe he did. Because twenty years later when I moved out there I had to call in alligator trappers.

I always had great birthday parties at the cabin. Standing on the banks with bamboo poles, we fished all afternoon and then fried the fish for supper. The year we had a spend-the-night party, Gary Paulk gave me a .22 rifle and I got to wear makeup for the first time. I wore powder blue eye shadow, midnight blue mascara, and shiny pink lipstick. We danced, and then the boys retired to the cow pasture with dad-chaperons and the girls stayed in the cabin with mom-chaperons. In the morning, we were all worn out from not sleeping because of the ghost stories and the boys sneaking around outside, making noises at the windows.

Twice there were blizzards on my birthday. I can understand a Kansas blizzard in late March, but when snow starts blowing in horizontal waves over a South Georgia pond and the wind breaks the pine trees in half, I have to wonder if I'm really where I think I am.

The March Sunday when a winter storm ripped through Georgia, my black and white streetwise cat Sport stopped eating. It was cold in the cabin, but she lay hunched on a metal table and didn't move when I called her. She didn't move when I offered her a treat, either, and her green eyes were glassy. I put my ear to her back. Her breathing was ragged. Somehow she had gotten suddenly very sick, and I was going to have to get her to the animal emergency room thirty miles away. In driving snow I walked to Gene's house across the road and he came down with his chain saw and removed the tree that had blown down across the driveway so I could get Sport to the vet.

She had pneumonia, I discovered. Worse, she also had leukemia. Two days later, when the weather was mild again, I had her put to sleep. I didn't hold her while she died, didn't even stay in the room with her. I waited in the lobby like a coward, wondering if the heartbreak would kill me.

My other birthday blizzard was in northeastern Kansas, while I was on retreat in a hermitage in the woods. I didn't know the snow was coming. It was chilly when I went to bed, but it didn't seem stormy. When I woke up the next morning, the porch on my hut was blanketed in six inches of fresh snow, and the only sound was of trees creaking under the wind and the weight of the continuing fall. When I hiked across the pasture and stood at the top of the hill, all I could see for miles was purest white. The sky was white, the ground, the roofs of houses, even the air was white with sparkling flakes that *luffed* down and drifted and piled in the fields and along the fence lines for the rest of the day.

🏠 Today I'm thirty-nine. The south wind is blowing hard but it's warm and the sun is out and the sky is that light blue shade of early spring. The question is, how am I going to celebrate? I think I'll go pull up some of those wild onions growing in the woods. I can make a whole salad out of the yard, with some dandelion greens, wild mustard, wild onions, a sprinkle of peppergrass.

Or maybe I'll drive to town and pick up Chinese. Broccoli chicken. With hot chili sauce. Hot-and-sour soup on the side.

Hey. Maybe I'll bake myself a cake. A chocolate cake with chocolate fudge icing. I can even get out my cake decorator set and write my name on top in little yellow roses, and "Happy Birthday!" with an exclamation point, the way MaRe taught me. I can put on thirty-nine yellow candles.

I know, I know: Jack Benny was always thirty-nine. But I only plan to be thirty-nine once. I don't want to miss anything.

Ample Fanny

I don't look in the mirror much any more. I don't wear makeup except on special occasions, and when I go to the grocery store or take the dogs to the vet, sometimes I forget to notice what I look like before I leave. So I might not know that my earrings don't match or that there's scrambled egg on my chin unless I see my reflection in a window, and then I'm surprised. Which can be fun, but it's not a practice I recommend, because of the ample fanny debacle.

In my teens I ran away from my first attempt at college to marry a dental student and move to Minneapolis. I worked as an insurance clerk so we could buy groceries, rent a patchwork leather sofa from Levitz, and keep gas in our orange Gremlin. One day during lunch, my friend Ruth and I went shopping downtown, and while she visited a public restroom I walked down the street and looked in the windows.

Soon I was startled by a commotion going on in the direction I'd just come from. Horns were blowing, and drivers were passing me with grins on their faces, craning their necks to look back.

I turned around, wondering what they were looking at, when I saw Ruth's ample fanny moving toward the restroom as fast as her high heels could clatter. The hem of her skirt was caught in the band of her panty hose, revealing her bottom to the world, and she was trailing five feet of toilet paper, which she was trying to snatch up as she ran.

So there's something to be said for looking in a mirror, if it's only to check your ample fanny.

Ski Bunny on the Threshold of Middle Age;
or, It's All Downhill from Here

*A*s I'd expected, the sharp slope where my Kansas drive-way met the gravel road was impossible for my Honda after a freak winter storm dumped eight inches of snow on a sheet of ice. I was heading to town for the mail when halfway up the hill the tires spun to a stop, and no amount of cursing or groaning or racing of the engine could keep the car from slid-ing back down. The windchill was at twenty below zero even though the day was sunny, and when I saw I was going to have to shovel my way up to the road, I backed the car down the quarter-mile track to the house so I could change from my thin jeans and sweater into real cold-weather clothes.

For years I'd been dragging around a one-piece ski bunny outfit my third ex-husband Terry had bought me on a Colo-rado ski trip when I was twenty-four. It was navy blue, a good shade for my blue eyes, with a zippered front, a smart turned-up collar, and hot pink racing stripes on the sleeves. It hugged my figure like a cat suit out of my Victoria's Secret catalogue. I wore a hot pink turtleneck under it, which lent my cheeks just the right amount of color.

Terry was a handsome man, tall and dark-haired and hazel-eyed, and he knew it, and I've always thought he bought me that ski bunny outfit so that I and my long blond hair would better complement his good looks. But I liked it anyway, which is why I still had it after fifteen years and the inevitable succession of changing body shapes that have accompanied me to the threshold of middle age.

But at twenty-four I was a good bit more slender than I am now, and when I pulled on that ski bunny outfit so I could shovel my Kansas driveway, I had to lie down on the bed to zip it up. When I walked, I couldn't bend my knees because the bottom half stuck to me like foil on a chewing gum wrapper, and as for wearing anything under it, well, I didn't own anything that thin. When I sat on the bed, my legs stuck straight out like matchsticks. If I stretched my arms all the way out, I could reach my feet just enough to pull on two pairs of wool socks and my oversize hiking boots. When I looked at myself in the mirror, I looked like a tall fat-footed duck.

I didn't really have to go to town that morning and get the mail; I could have waited until the next day. But what if I'd won a sweepstakes or something? I'm always looking for money to come in the mail. Sometimes it does. My insurance company is mutually owned, so every five or six years I get a check for fifteen dollars.

So, clad for winter, now I goose-stepped to the car and, puffing, heaved in the snow shovel, folded myself behind the steering wheel, and drove back to the bottom of the slope. Half an hour later, I'd dug down to gravel halfway up the hill, and I got back in the car and gunned the engine and managed to skid to the top of the driveway.

I decided to get some sand from the hardware store to pour over the snow, not wanting to slide into the pond on the way back down the driveway. This meant I had to expose my ski bunny outfit to the men in the hardware store. I pretended not to notice the glances that (I'm sure) followed my progress to the back of the building, where the sandbags were stacked on the floor. I bought four, which a smirking (I'm sure he was smirking) teenage boy, one of those hulking football-player types, carried to the car for me.

At the post office, I didn't get any money in the mail, but I did get my new Victoria's Secret catalogue. There were some twenty-four-year-old black leather and red satin ski bunnies in it. They made me so mad that I went in and showed them to Elmer, the postman, who's about ready to retire. I slapped the catalogue down on the counter. "I want you to look at this, Elmer," I said, flipping through the lace panties and silk teddies. "These are the skinniest women alive."

"Uh-huh," mumbled Elmer.

"And people are surprised that all our children are anorexic."

"That's right," said Elmer.

"Can you believe this, Elmer?" I said, pointing to a gorgeous brunette in a black minidress who looked six feet tall and had a waist the size of my calf. "How can she live like that?"

Elmer cleared his throat. "Well, that's . . . that's just a . . . a *shame!*" he said.

I left the catalogue with Elmer and stormed back out to the car.

What I hadn't realized, I saw when I got back to my driveway, was that the sandbags weighed seventy pounds, which was more weight than I could lift out of the back of my car, especially considering that I was so . . . squeezed in. Now, how was I going to get that sand out of those bags and onto the snow?

I spied a Wendy's cup that had been rolling around for several weeks on the floor of the car. Aha, I thought. That's it. I dipped the cup into one of the bags and sprinkled the sand over the driveway, then dipped it into the bag again and sprinkled some more. I did this until the bag was light enough for me to hold.

It was way after lunchtime before I'd emptied all four bags of sand; but finally, exhausted and cold, I finished the job. Then I scrunched back into the car and drove down the hill to the house.

The next day the temperature rose to fifty-five degrees and melted all the snow, and the sand became part of the driveway.

Goin' Nekkid

My beard grows to my toes,
I never wears no clothes,
I wraps my hair
Around my bare,
And down the road I goes.

Shel Silverstein

*N*ekkid is how we say it in Georgia.

I first got acquainted with public nakedness with my Italian boyfriend. His Kansas City friends had a hot tub outside on their deck, which sidled up beneath the trees in their back yard. On an icy night in January, when the snow was four inches thick on the grass and the night was black and starfilled, I was invited into the hot tub with all these people *sans vêtements.* Not wanting to appear startled (which I was) or unsophisticated (which I was), I made the mistake of affecting an apparent lazy carelessness for so long that by the time I sauntered onto the deck, everybody else had already found their places on the benches under the water. Now all they had left to do was watch me undress.

I stood shivering in my bare feet, peeling off a layer of clothing at a time while the happy crowd looked on, fearing that my inability to unhook my bra or something was going to brand me as gauche for life. Of course they were looking. I knew they were looking even though they seemed to disregard me completely, laughing and chatting about things unrelated to nakedness, like politics (well, maybe not entirely unrelated) and the weather, and holding their martinis out of the water, while the steam rose and wavered around them like heat devils off hot pavement.

They *had* to be looking. *I* would have been looking. Where I grew up, people were always looking. If you wore the same dress to church two Sundays in a row, people talked about it in the beauty shop on Monday. Deciding what blouse went with what skirt, which earrings might be "too much," which pocketbook matched your shoes, whether wearing jeans would be tacky—and seeing how other people looked, whether their stockings were taupe when they should have been nude or their hair was too heavily frosted or their mascara was too thick—it's the southern pastime, as American as baseball.

But I pretended not to notice all the naked people gawking at my pale naked body with the legs that were great, as my first ex-husband had put it, from the knee down, and into the tub I stepped, holding my martini with an awkward indifference, and sat down.

I stared around me, gathering in the details, curious about these people who could climb in and out of the tub on a whim, sit on the edge when they got too hot, or go inside and pour fresh drinks, chat, turn around and laugh, walk away, walk back, without seeming to care whether their butts were flabby or their penises flopped against their legs when they walked or their makeup was running or their proportions were two by four or thirty-six by thirty-six. I couldn't get it. Didn't they feel silly? Exposed? *Nekkid?*

I pictured all the things I disliked about my body, my life, my self hanging off me like parasitic fish on a whale's belly. It reminded me of a documentary I saw on public television once where some budding entrepreneur had caught a dolphin, tied a plastic alligator to his tail, and put him out to pasture in a dirty bywater where you could pay fifty cents to watch him swim around. Wherever he went, so did the alligator.

Nevertheless, after the martini, the shock began to wear off and I got around to noticing other things—the easy camaraderie among these friends, the lack of pretense in their conversation, the warmth of their laughter, and beyond them, the darkness, the moon I could catch only a glimpse of behind the trees, the strains of soft jazz from inside, and at last the comfort of a hot bath on a winter night. Eventually, that other people were in there with me didn't matter so much any more, and I stopped looking at them and realized that they probably weren't looking at me, after all, and that, to my surprise, they weren't going to be losing sleep over the size of my thighs. Now that was a shock.

🏠All this exposure with the Italian made life with my third ex-husband Terry less dramatic than it would have been otherwise. Before we got our own hot tub, our neighbors had theirs, and because they lived at the end of the cul-de-sac half a dozen townhouses down from ours, they sometimes dared us to walk home after their parties *au naturel.* They'd stand in the yard and howl with laughter while we strolled up the hill in the night with our jeans bundled under our arms, admonishing each other not to run. Sometimes the whole party would relocate to the swimming pool after it closed and there we'd all be, thirty of us, fat, tall, skinny, sixtyish, twentyish, bald, hairy, and shaved, sneaking over the locked wrought-iron gate like truants, skinny-dipping until the wee hours.

So I came to discover that there's no freedom like the feel of water enveloping a naked body, and once I could ignore enough of my hang-ups to try it, I was hooked forever. This doesn't mean I've turned into a nudist or that I go parading around bare-breasted on French beaches, but only that, if I get the chance to go unencumbered into a pool, I'll more than likely risk it.

Sometimes the risks run on the high side, like when Terry and I canoed naked for half an hour down the Buffalo River in Arkansas. Without a soul out there but us, the season being late fall, we wanted to see how canoeing naked would feel. Then Terry put me out on a rock in the middle of the river and paddled away by himself. A few minutes later he paddled back, Odysseus charmed by the Siren. He thought that was pretty funny. I got a sunburn.

•

I once told Mom that sometimes I run through the yard without clothes on and she didn't handle that very well, but I told her that I wasn't showing anything to anybody but God and God already knew what I looked like. Early on a summer morning, I might streak to the sauna to put dog food in the bowl, too lazy to put my pajamas on after I've thrust them off, too hot, in the night.

I have a friend in Georgia whose back yard is separated from her neighbor's only by a thin hedge, but still some days she stands naked in the rain like a birdbath in a garden, collecting water in her hair and letting it drip down her body.

Kelly walks around her house all the time without clothes on, finding them too troublesome to bother with. She's a catlike person, long and flexible and sensual.

I remember once when I still owned my paralegal business seeing a group of people in a conference room, giving depositions to a court reporter. They were buttoned up to the chins in suits. I was dressed like that, too, in my linen jacket and floral skirt, my stockings and high heels. It reminded me how I preferred to be outdoors.

After that I started dressing more casually for the office, sometimes even daring myself to leave off my makeup. That was a trial. On those days, people asked me if I felt all right. "You look really tired," they'd say. Or, "Gosh, you look pale." Or, "Are your eyes all right? They look kind of pinched up."

"Oh, I'm just not wearing any makeup," I'd say.

"Why not?" they'd ask, frowning.

The question was too hard to answer. "It's still me," I'd tell them.

But I do my friends the same way. At a conference a few months ago I said to my friend Tricia, "Hmmm. You look different today than yesterday."

"Oh," she said, her face reddening. "I'm just not wearing any makeup."

🏠Now I'm still self-conscious about the stretch marks from when I gained thirty-five pounds as a teenager and the way my thighs bulge under my drooping derriere and the way the fat lies in cellulitic globs above my knees. And having what Mom calls "chubby little legs" does not dispose me to show them off as if I were a five-foot version of Shirley MacLaine.

Years ago, my therapist made me stand before an imaginary mirror and pretend I was naked. I had to describe myself to him. It was awful. I wanted to die right there and bleed all over his office and leave permanent stains.

But now sometimes on hot days I sit in the study without a shirt on, like today, and the wild white roses in the blue porcelain vase that my friend Red Crow made are setting up a sweet scent that I can smell all over the house. Outside the chapel window, a red-headed woodpecker drills the west wall, and chickadees gather in the hickories.

Corrupting Mama

My mother never was one to color outside the lines. I, her headstrong and thoroughly independent eldest daughter, always have been, and it's a wonder she survived it, she being from the Deep South where a daughter was not under any circumstances, at any age, to act unladylike, be discourteous, exhibit bad manners, dress inappropriately, or break rules. It would be too embarrassing.

Here's how it goes:

I buy so many clothes at a department store that I startle the manager by asking for a price break. "How about a price break for cash?" I say.

Mama, standing behind me, gasps in horror. "Amy, that's rude! Please excuse her!" she says to the manager. She grabs my elbow and ushers me out of the store. I am twenty-eight at the time, going through my third divorce.

"Honey, you can't park here. This isn't a parking place."
"I'm making my own, Mama."
Mama gasps in horror, looks around anxiously for the Parking Police.

"Amy, honey. You're not going to wear *that,* I hope."

At Christmas dinner before the family is seated I trade my salad for my cousin's because hers has more croutons on it. Mama slaps my hand. "Amy! Put that back!" she says. "That's bad manners!"
"Mama, I'm not twelve." (I'm thirty-seven.)
"But you're still my *child.*"

"Don't sit like that, honey. It's unladylike."

"Amy. Hold your shoulders up."

What it is, Mom's afraid I'm going to get caught and she'll have to explain me to her friends.
Supreme Judge of Southern Decorum: "Amy Blackmarr, we've caught you at last! I'm sentencing you to Life at Hard Labor for . . . EMBARRASSING YOUR MOTHER!"
Gallery (full of Mom's friends plus some people she's destined to meet in the future): Gasps of horror.
Mama: Flashes the gallery an apologetic look.

So when I tell Mom that QUESTION AUTHORITY is my favorite bumper sticker, she looks heavenward and sighs. I don't say anything about the UPPITY WOMEN UNITE bumper sticker she had on her Honda until she traded it in and when she couldn't get the bumper sticker off without ruining it bought a new one for her big maraschino-cherry-colored Toyota.

Mom was terrific help when I moved back to Kansas. She's a great organizer because she likes for things to be IN ORDER. I always like to have her along in a chaotic situation, because she's an expert at putting things back where they belong.

When Mom comes visiting, right away she gets the broom and starts sweeping. If she finds something distasteful, like a roach or a dirty bathtub, she makes a sound of utter disgust like, "*Oh,* Lord," and immediately corrects the offense. She straightens whatever's on my dresser and my bathroom shelves. At Kelly's house Mom washes the dishes, empties the litter box, and Sani-Flushes the toilets. If we leave letters or bills or notes lying around, Mom has the courtesy to read them before putting them away so she knows where they go in the house. She's handy that way. When I was fourteen she once tried to put me back in order by reading my diary, but I didn't appreciate it much at the time.

Now I'm forty and I don't hide anything from my mother

because frankly, after her divorce and Kelly's and all three of mine, I think her embarrassment nerves are getting dull.

🏠I used to watch Mitch Miller on television when I was little. One night the camera zoomed in on a saxophone player in the band. All of a sudden he whipped his head around and where I expected to see the back of his head was another face. The face was so real it scared me, even though I understood that it had to be a mask.

I never could figure out how he did that, switched one face for the other so fast, like a magician's sleight of hand. Sleight of face. "I've grown accustomed to her face," the song says. You get used to a face.

🏠Public bathrooms make me cringe. I don't like other people's smells, their pale yellow droplets on the toilet seat, their crumpled toilet paper on the floor that didn't make it into the bowl. So in a department store or a restaurant I sneak into the employees' bathroom if I can get in without a key.

Mama thinks this is terrible. She's afraid I'll get hauled up before the management and paddled, or something. I don't know.

But on the trip up to Kansas from Georgia, my mother sneaked into an employees' bathroom behind me. At first I didn't know she was there—I thought she'd gone into the public bathroom. So it shocked me when she emerged from the toilet stall at my back while I was standing in front of the mirror washing my hands. "Mom?" I said. "Mother?"

"You were right, Amy," she said, smoothing her shorts. "This is a lot more . . . pleasant."

She took her time getting out of there. I kept a nervous watch out for the Toilet Authorities, but we got away clean. I didn't tell her how relieved I was about that.

The next thing I knew, Mama was helping me sneak Max into a hotel room. We were dead tired one night because we'd been unloading all day long, but we had no place to sleep because I hadn't put the bed together yet. So we put Max in the car and drove to Lawrence and checked in at the Ramada. It was around midnight. Mom didn't ask the desk clerk if dogs were allowed, and I didn't, either, because Max is never a problem in a hotel room anyway. He's quiet and house-trained and not too hairy, but how was I going to explain that to a desk clerk?

As we were walking back to the car I whispered to Mom, "What about Max?"

She looked at me and shrugged.

"But, Mama," I said, "we can't just leave him in the car all night."

"We'll have to sneak him in," she said as she slid into her seat and I gaped at her, remembering *Invasion of the Body Snatchers* and wondering if she'd touched one of those pods and just not told me about it.

It was a huge motel, and thank goodness our room was a

long way from the office. I parked the car and leashed Max.
Mom was point man. She crossed the parking lot, scouting,
then slipped inside the glass door and looked around. In a
minute she came to the door and signaled me to advance.

I skittered across the lot with Max, except that just before
we reached the door Mom started making hand motions for
me to *go back, go back!* I looked around for somewhere to
hide and spied a box shrub a few feet from the entrance. I
dragged Max behind it and crouched down just as this blond
woman showed up and started talking to Mom. They stood
there and stood there, and I waited and waited behind that
bush, which was two feet wide by two feet tall and didn't
hide either Max or me anyway, I being in plain view from
the shoulders up and Max and I both in plain view from the
shins down should the woman decide to glance to her left,
and I couldn't believe that my mother was having this *conversation* with this woman while Max and I were hanging out
like crooks in the shrubbery.

Finally I got so fed up I stepped out from behind the bush
and marched back across the parking lot with Max. If the
woman tells on me, I thought, so be it.

A few minutes later Mom appeared. "I'm sorry, honey,
but that was the *night manager,*" she told me. "I couldn't think
of anything to do but occupy her attention. She's gone now."

This time I swept Max up in my arms and Mom and I
both ran back across the parking lot, into the building, up the
stairs, and down the hall to our room, the last in a long string
of rooms, my heart thumping the whole time.

After we got settled, Mom went to get a Coke and spotted two men sneaking a puppy down the hall under blankets.

The next morning when she went to the front desk for coffee, she saw a man with a poodle in the lobby.

A few days later Mom turned into a dumpster criminal, and that's when I lost track of her altogether.

She wanted to wait until after sunset to do the job—that is, to steal dumpster space. I had nowhere to throw away my carload of empty boxes and the other inevitable trash that piles up when you move into a place, and I didn't have a garbage man, and all we could think of was to sneak down to the Midland Farm Store and "borrow" their dumpster, which was against the law. That didn't stop Mama. By the time the sun dropped below the horizon she was shuttling me down the gravel road in the car. Before I knew it, we were tiptoeing back and forth from the car to the dumpster with our heads ducked, trying to stay out of the headlights from passing cars and hoping none of them belonged to the sheriff.

Who is this person out robbing dumpster space with me? I was thinking.

I was thinking, My mother's gone off somewhere and left behind a xerox.

Last week, Mom went to the Middle East with a handful of artists and theologians on some kind of spiritual quest; I'm not sure what exactly. Right now my mother is walking past armed guards in Syrian streets, riding a camel through the desert in the middle of the night, climbing Mount Sinai, or getting blown up on a bus by terrorists on a jihad. I'm pretty sure she didn't take her makeup.

Every morning I look at her itinerary to see where she is—Syria, Jordan, Israel, Egypt—and I think, such a risk she's taking. Besides, the water. She's supposed to tape over the taps so she won't accidentally brush her teeth in the water. I wonder if she remembered.

Today I tried to call her in Jerusalem to see how she was getting along, but the people there couldn't find her name on the guest register. I left her a message, but she never did call me back.

Grasshopper

$\mathcal{I}$'d had my plane reservations for six months.

The night before I was supposed to fly out of Kansas City for the Georgia conference, I set the clock and the coffeepot, which are both beside my bed, for six in the morning, three hours before flight time.

At midnight on a nervous impulse I reset them both for five.

I'd already taken the dogs to the kennel. My packed suitcase was by the kitchen door with my pocketbook. My clothes for the flight were ironed and laid out on a chair.

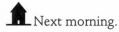Next morning.

The sound of birds singing.

Broad yellow daylight, streaming in through the south windows.

I grabbed the clock: it was after seven-thirty! The alarm hadn't rung! The coffee had perked, but I'd been sleeping too hard for it to wake me, and now it had already sat there for two hours and shut itself off. Aaaggh!

The coffee was cold and my mind was numb. I'd never missed a plane in my life. I'm usually too early for everything. Now I had an appointment in Atlanta at three and a panel to chair the next morning, and people were counting on me, and I was still an hour away from the airport.

I gulped down cold coffee and called Mom in Georgia. "I'm about to miss my plane," I said, close to tears.

"Oh, honey. Where are you?"

"I'm still at home. I set the alarm for p.m. instead of a.m."

"Amy, I can't believe it. That's so unlike you."

"I know."

"You're generally so organized."

"I know."

"I wonder what happened."

"I have no idea."

"You must have some unconscious fear of going to this conference."

"Good grief, Mom."

"Oh, you're in luck," said the Delta agent when I called the airport. "Your plane's right on time."

Aaaggh!

I threw off my pajamas, pulled on my clothes, grabbed my bags, and dashed to the car. On the way to the airport, I almost ran over a wild turkey and some rabbits. By the time I boarded the shuttle to the terminal, the plane had left.

I raced to the pay phone to call my travel agent. But it was a long-distance call, and I didn't have a phone card yet.

"You can use any credit card but Visa," the operator said.

"But that's all I've got left," I said. "I cut up the Master-Cards so I wouldn't go bankrupt."

"Can't you make a collect call?"

"Not to my travel agent. Can I charge the calls to my home number?"

"Is there someone there to okay the charges?"

"*I'm* okaying the charges."

"I have to speak to someone at the residence."

"Lady, if I were at home, I wouldn't be HERE. Listen," I said, bursting into tears. "I've got money in the bank and money in my wallet and credit EVERYWHERE. All I want to do is—"

"Oh, honey, now don't cry," said the operator. "Surely we can think of somebody you can charge a call to. What about your mother?"

"Her office won't accept collect calls." I sniffed and thought about it. "We could try my dad and stepmother."

"Sure we can. Now, it's going to be all right," said the operator. "We'll find somebody." She was so warm and kind that I could almost feel her arm around my shoulders. The idea gave me comfort, gave me breathing room, and I found a Kleenex in my pocketbook and blew my nose while she dialed Dad's number.

Thank heaven, my stepmother was home. She told the operator that I could charge a call to her number. I called my mom and charged it to my stepmother. Then I called my stepmother back to explain what was going on and charged it to my mom. I ignored the fact that the two women had barely spoken to each other in twenty years.

When I finally reached my travel agent, every seat to Atlanta on every airline was taken. Road Atlanta had begun, and everybody was going to the races.

At the ticket counter, the Delta agent told me, "Oh, you can go on standby. I'm sure you'll be able to make one of the next few flights."

The ten o'clock flight went out overbooked by nine passengers.

The lunchtime flights went out overbooked by fifteen passengers.

The early afternoon flight went out overbooked by nineteen passengers and a long line of standbys. We looked at each other and shrugged. I went back to the ticket counter.

"You don't stand a chance of getting on any flight as a standby today," said the new ticket agent. "They're all overbooked."

"I've noticed," I said.

"There's one seat left on the last flight out tonight. It's first class. That's all I can do."

"How much?"

"Four hundred dollars, in addition to what you've already paid. That's one-way."

"My round-trip ticket was only a hundred and fifty!"

He shrugged.

I handed over my Visa card.

At seven-thirty, I sat down in my five-hundred-dollar seat, first row, first class. For my money I got a little more leg room, all the complimentary Bloody Marys I could hold, a turkey sandwich on a bagel, and an overly solicitous flight attendant. The peons in third class got peanuts and had to pay three dollars for their vodka and press a button when they wanted anything.

We touched down in Atlanta half an hour late. By the time I reached the rental car counter where I had a reservation, it was midnight. I still had to drive two hundred miles.

The rental car counter was empty. I went next door to Avis. No cars. Everybody going to the races.

Next door to Budget. No cars.

Next door where a dozen other people were waiting. Some of them I recognized from my flight. When I stepped into the line, one of the two agents helping people took his carton of Chinese food and with a grand sigh disappeared into a back room, leaving the other woman to handle the customers on her own.

I got on the road around one. Under a bridge on the way out of town I sat in the car for an hour while a wreck was cleared away. Fortunately, I wasn't in it.

A few hours later, I was early to my conference panel.

•

Driving back to the house of steps from the airport the following week I was going eighty miles an hour down the interstate when I noticed a grasshopper the size of my thumb on the hood, hunkered down over its angled legs, its barbed feet dug into a mud spot. Somehow it was hanging on in that torrent, shifting its weight from side to side while the wind streamed and surged around it like a herd of antelope skirting a solitary tree on a prairie.

I was wondering what the world must look like to a grasshopper going light speed down the interstate on the hood of a car. Where the heck am I? it was probably thinking. I knew that feeling, of hanging on by my fingernails while life whizzed past, blasting away what little understanding I may have come to.

The grasshopper survived all fifty miles, despite a brief stop at a traffic light where it turned sideways to the wind and got airlifted to the windshield when we took off again. It landed upside down with its head behind the wiper blade. But after a few minutes it managed to right itself, and it rode the rest of the way with its antennae straight up. As I turned down the driveway, I thought, What irony, if Red eats this grasshopper as soon as it hits the ground.

Endurance, says Caroline Myss, makes the soul come up to the surface. I've been through worse than a missed airplane. I've been through deaths, divorces, betrayals, failures, and disappointments. But they all add up to the same thing. I don't like the way it feels to realize I'm at the mercy of the universe. It lays me out too thin, makes me feel brittle, like if somebody knocked me down I'd break in half. Times like those, what I think I know about life, about myself, about the way the world works, gets turned inside out. Suddenly I'm not the capable adult who can handle any crisis, but only a child left orphaned in an airport, feeling helpless in an unfamiliar world, and only a stranger's kindness can give me room to recollect my ordinary self.

The Big Game

*A*ll my dogs are limping. Floyd's limping on his front foot, Red's limping in back, and now Max's straight-up ear has flopped, having been bitten into, torn through, clipped off, and stitched. Max is always proving himself against some ferocious beast. This time a bobcat gnawed on his head and broke some arteries that gushed blood all over Max, the deck, the blanket in my car, and the vet's office.

But Max is dauntless. Right now he's chasing cicadas in the cut grass, snapping them up like popcorn with a satisfied look on his scarred face, the threads from his stitches sticking out like tiny cowlicks. Floyd and Red watch him placidly from the shade.

I grew up playing games. I played Monopoly with Daddy, Perquacky with Kelly, Pictionary with my cousins, and rummy with our baby-sitter, Granny Griffin. I played poker, pitch, Twister, Scrabble, and the Game of Life. All day long on Sundays MaRe and I played canasta. Now I play Free Cell on my computer and blackjack at the casinos, and the pit bosses say I play a perfect game. But I'm a terrible gambler, because I like the game so much I play too long and give back all my winnings.

On vacation in the Florida Gulf I went looking for a seashell to bring back to Joe, because I knew he loved the ocean. Coral would be just right, I thought, and soon I found a pure white piece of coral. Delighted, I put it in my pocket and felt satisfied it was the perfect gift. I walked on.

Then I found another piece of coral, larger and whiter than the first. I put it in my pocket, too, unsure now which one to give away.

Soon after that I found a black rock that looked interesting, and a purple scallop shell, and a lightning whelk and a turkey wing and a boat shell. It wasn't long before my pocket was bulging with perfect gifts.

When I got back to the cottage where I was staying, I spread everything out on the breakfast table. I took each rock, shell, and bit of coral into my hand and turned it over, felt it, thought about it, tried to decide which one Joe would like best. I finally decided on the second piece of coral I'd found, and I laid it on a paper towel by itself, away from the other things. Then I made tacos and turned on the news.

All evening I was aware of that piece of coral on the paper towel. The more I thought about it, the more I doubted my choice. Maybe Joe would like something else after all.

The next morning, I awoke with the decision to give Joe the first piece of coral, instead of the second one. It seemed the simplest choice. This was the best gift; I was certain. Joe was always reminding me to simplify.

By lunch I'd decided on the whelk, and after that I decided on some shells I found later.

At one point I decided not to give him anything. He wouldn't care anyway.

It wasn't until I got back to Kansas with all of my perfect gifts that I resolved once and for all to give Joe the first piece of coral I'd found. When I went to see him, he took the coral in his hand and held it for a long time. He didn't say a word.

Shoot, I thought. I *knew* he'd rather have that other one.

Finally he smiled. "You see, Amy," he said, "there's competition even among rocks."

My dad taught me: "Strive for perfection."

"But Dad," I'd say. "Only God is perfect."

"Nevertheless. *Strive,*" Dad would say. "Do more; do your best; do the most you can possibly do. You owe it to yourself and to God to live up to your potential."

So I drive home eight different ways, to find the one that's fastest. I push-mow a half acre of yard, run six miles instead of three, spend an hour on a single sentence, getting the sound of it right. Living up to my potential: it's the Ultimate Competition, the Cosmic Challenge, the Big Game; and like a blister beetle it trespasses over all the planted fields of my life, gobbling up shoots.

Insectomaniacs

$\mathcal{I}$ keep a bowl full of bugs in the bedroom. This woodsy hang-out harbors such a shocking variety of insects that I've started saving the dead ones. I got the idea from Aunt Helen, who thinks bugs are gorgeous.

In my bowl I have a Green Metallic Bee, tiny and iridescent, with crystalline wings. I have a Woolly Bear Moth with a white mane, an Ivory-Marked Beetle with forked toes and inch-long antennae, a pure white Fairy Moth, a pair of spindly-legged Crane Flies, and a yellow moth with pink stripes that I can't find in any of my books.

Insects are crazy. When I read in bed at night, giant Sphinx Moths bang against the window screens like bats. Painted Lady Butterflies love the UPS man, and they crowd around him like gnats as soon as his truck rolls to a stop and he shoves open the door. Blister Beetles hitchhike to flowers on the backs of bees—that is, if the Bee Assassins don't pounce on the bees and suck out their insides first. Black Widows dangle under outhouse seats and, after mating, eat their mates for a snack. The white legs of Phantom Crane Flies appear and disappear in bad light like ghosts. Jumping Spiders have eight eyes so they can see all the way around. When a Click Beetle lands upside down, it flips itself into the air with a *click!* and lands rightside up again.

Hunting wasps love the house of steps. Hunting wasps eat other insects. A female Cricket Hunter numbs a cricket with her stinger and then drags it into her nest and lays an egg on it. The larva chews into the cricket and eats its internal organs, which, eventually, kills the cricket. "Larva feeds initially on nonessential tissues," says my field guide. "Later eats indiscriminately, killing host." Then the larva pupates beside the carnage.

Some Cricket Hunters have an affinity for Mormon Crickets but don't like Jerusalem Crickets. Other hunting wasps prefer caterpillars or spiders. Tarantula Hawks like the taste of tarantulas.

Yellow Jackets carry away bits of your fried chicken at a picnic. Fishing Spiders hold their breath underwater for half an hour while eating tadpoles.

Besides being crazy, bugs have terrific names. Take the Blood-sucking Conenose, for instance. Or the Nebraska Cone-head. (Yes, really.)

There's The Jagged Ambush Bug. The Horse Lubber

Grasshopper (lubs horses). The Trapdoor Spider. The Big-headed Ant (they're so vain). The Little Black Antlion.

There's that Texas Shed-Builder Ant (builds sheds in Texas). That False Potato Beetle (eats false potatoes).

And how about those Black Witches? Those Pleasing Fungus Beetles? Those Silvery Checkerspots?

How about those Cow Killers? Spotted Camel Crickets? Long-horned Earwigs? Dog Faces? Hebrews?

Silverfishes. Fishflies. Sawflies. Scorpionflies. Dragonflies. Whiteflies. Stoneflies. Snakeflies. Owlflies.

Mealybugs. Pillbugs. Stilt Bugs. Splittlebugs. Bed Bugs. Stink Bugs.

Walkingsticks. Weevils. Whipscorpions. Whirligigs. Wood Nymphs.

Soldier Bugs. Sharpshooters. Water Boatmen. Back-swimmers.

Jagged-edged Saddlebags.

Eastern Toe-biters. Hmmm.

The Seventeen-Year and Thirteen-Year Cicadas all came out at once this year in Kansas, which like Halley's Comet is something that doesn't happen often. All summer long the sound of them was deafening. After a while, though, the racket stopped, and the larvae crept into holes in the ground to wait around for another thirteen or seventeen years. In two hundred and twenty-one years, they'll all come out together again and have a big party.

Each synchronized population of cicadas is called a

brood. Only fourteen broods of Seventeen-Year Cicadas and five broods of Thirteen-Year Cicadas are known to exist today. Now there are fewer than that, because of Max, who pretty much on his own decimated the Kansas cicada population. Max ate so many cicadas that, for a while, he got fat and round like a cicada himself. All day long he lay in the grass, puffing like a wormy puppy.

A movie called *Microcosmos* portrays the world of bugs from the bugs' point of view. An ornithologist I know told me that it would change my ideas about bugs forever, so last night I watched it. In the movie, mosquitoes look like angels, and caterpillars traveling in long lines all pulsate in the same rhythm like a single entity.

Meanwhile, in my yard, spiders hang suspended in silvery nighttime webs that stretch across the sky from redbud branch to walnut tree, and when I walk to the sauna, my head breaks through silk.

Pushing the River

Everything in its own time.

The Indigo Girls

*U*nder the eave on the sauna, a phoebe built a mossy nest on a window ledge. I discovered the nest in April, when the wine-colored tulips and blue phlox and yellow daffodils were blooming and I could smell the mint growing by the garden wall.

After I found the nest, I went out every day to watch what happened. Standing by a nearby hedge-apple tree I was just tall enough to see the top of the mother phoebe's head, which she moved in anxious jerks. Sometimes she flew to the bucket under the spigot, perched on the edge, and pecked at the water, drinking.

When she left in search of food I climbed up on a concrete block beneath the nest and looked inside. It held three eggs, one larger than the others. If the mother bird saw me near the nest, she flew to the branches of the hedge-apple and chirped at me until I went away.

The eggs hatched in May. The mother brought back bugs to feed the baby birds, but soon one was bigger than the others. I often found the bigger bird sitting on the little ones, who seemed weak and hungry.

One day I stood on the concrete block and cooed at the bigger bird, to see if it would move away from the others. Startled, it launched itself out of the nest and tumbled to the ground. The little birds lifted their heads and peeped, their open mouths as big as their heads.

I chased the fallen bird, clapping my hands, hurrying it away from Red, who was bounding through the yard toward us. The awkward baby could only fly for short spurts, but it managed to reach a low branch of the hedge-apple before Red could catch it.

The bigger bird never came back, and eventually the other two got fatter and grew feathers. But I got too close to the nest again one day and both little birds took off prematurely and flopped to the ground. Red came running. The mother phoebe darted from branch to branch, chirping. One baby made it safely into the tree. The other hopped off into the long grass, but this time I caught Red and sat him down, and the bird got away.

"Why do you walk so fast?" Mom asks, as I, several paces ahead, never seem to let her catch up.

"It's just my pace," I tell her, curious at my sense of urgency over nothing, which has plagued me all my life.

There's an electronic game on my computer called Minesweeper where I have to clear all the mines out of the blocks while the clock's ticking. I can do the smallest game in six seconds.

I'm always forgetting. I once left a turkey roasting in the oven and went out for an afternoon walk. When I got back, around sunset, the turkey had shrunk to a chicken. I left a two-pound roast in the oven once for four hours and it cooked itself into a brick.

I can't count the times I've turned on the stove to boil water for tea and burned up the pot. It seems the instant I turn on the burner I forget about it. Once I put on a pot of water and then wrote myself a note to come back and check on it in a few minutes. I took the note upstairs and stuck it on the computer, where I was working. Half an hour later, when I smelled the pot burning, I saw the note.

The same thing happens when I clean house. I start washing the kitchen counters but then I find a hair clamp that belongs in the bathroom so I take the clamp into the bathroom and then I notice the bathtub needs scouring so I pour in the Comet and turn on the water and while I'm waiting for the tub to soak I remember that I left my earrings in the den so I run upstairs to get them and notice that the trash can needs emptying so I think I'll just do this one little chore but I end up emptying all the trash cans in the house including the one in the kitchen which is when I remember I still haven't finished washing the kitchen counters. Everything gets done; it just gets done in spurts. I call this activity Spontaneous Housework.

The scary thing is that I'm barely middle-aged and I'm already having to feel the toothbrush to see if it's wet because I can't remember whether I've brushed my teeth.

I'm sure that some days I've put on deodorant more than twice.

Once I got all the way to the vet before I remembered I'd left the dogs at home.

This forgetfulness is a family trait. MaRe, in a frantic hurry, pulled into a gas station one day and told the attendant to fill up the tank, then drove off yelling that she'd be back in a minute to get the car.

Driving through a parking lot, my mother once absent-mindedly threw her car into reverse.

My dad writes down everything I tell him and puts it in a file so he won't forget it, then forgets where he put the file or even whether he wrote anything down in the first place.

Sometimes I get stop signs mixed up with traffic lights, and I sit in the car waiting for the stop sign to turn green.

Kelly, well, she just lives in Kelly-time.

I think we're a very distracted family.

When I was twelve, my dad would come into my room early in the morning before school and whisper, "Mornin', sweetheart. You goin' to walk with me?"

"Already?" I'd grumble, reluctant to leave my warm blankets for the South Georgia February chill that lay in ambush for me on the other side of our front door, that somehow went straight through to my bones no matter how many layers I wore.

But I'd look up at my dad, framed in the doorway from the light down the hall, and giggle at the flaps on his furry hat that came down over his ears, and crawl out of bed because I couldn't stand to disappoint him.

It was never a long walk, a couple of miles at most. We had two routes, and part of the fun was deciding which one to take on those cold mornings. On days when time was short, we'd take the road past the farmers' cold storage, which always smelled like bacon.

On mornings when we didn't have to hurry, we'd go east from our front porch, angle northward, and walk by the pastured horse and the open fields where the dirt was turned up, awaiting spring planting. We'd turn back toward town at the Red & White Grocery Store. The sun would be up by then, casting a pale light over the day.

But both routes led to our destination: the Osceola Restaurant across the street from the Baptist church, where Geraldine in her white waitress uniform was serving scrambled eggs and keeping the coffee hot. I loved to open that glass door and hear the bell jingle on the other side, to step out of a steely morning into that warm yellow room and find myself gathered in by the talk and laughter of the farmers and merchants clustered around the tables, who held with rough, strong hands their white ceramic cups of steaming coffee.

"Mr. Vernon, Mr. Charles," Daddy would say, nodding, "you doin' all right this morning?"

"We're doin' all right," they'd say. "You doin' all right, Mr. Rudy?"

"Fine, fine," Daddy would say.

"How you doin', sweetheart?" Mr. Charles might ask.

"Just fine, fine," I'd say, and Dad and I would sit down to coffee—or for me it was hot chocolate—in brown paper cups that made your hands too hot, because we only had time for a powdered sugar doughnut and a word with Geraldine, who was always happy to see us.

On the way home, Daddy would philosophize.

"All in the world you need to be happy, sweetie pie," he'd say, swinging his walking stick, "is an orange crate to sit on and your self-respect. And if you had to," he'd add, "you could do without—"

"—the orange crate!" I'd finish, and we'd laugh.

I never wanted those walks to end. They were a stretch of calm water for me, far removed from the turbulent thoughts of a troubled girl on the threshold of pubescence.

But I could have enjoyed them more if as soon as we got outdoors I hadn't started worrying about coming back. "What time is it, Daddy?" I'd ask the minute we set foot on the road. "Let's don't come back for a long time. Let's go the long way." I was so busy warding off time, I scarcely noticed the frost on the grass or the ice at the edges of the mud puddles or our frozen breath in the winter air.

•

Don't push the river, wrote Barry Stevens; it flows by itself. But even now I still do it, still try to get time off my back. Last Saturday Sara and her husband Carl came to my house for a cheese soup supper and we had such fun that the whole time I was thinking, Please don't go home yet. Please don't go home yet. I tried living without clocks but it made me nervous, like a restaurant bell always poised in suspension, waiting for the door to open.

It seems I've always been in a hurry, getting too far ahead, or maybe running to catch up with all the years I'm afraid are slipping away like the color of maples at the end of October. But now I'm wondering if those years have been behind me all this time, trying to grab my sleeve and make me turn around. Maybe I left them in my childhood—look! there they are still, settled peacefully into those winter morning walks with my dad, alive in our first glimpse of twilight as we stepped out-of-doors, and in the warmth of a gloved hand on my back, guiding me forward.

Buried Hardware

. . . my own soul, plowed into the garden.

Marck L. Beggs

I've been chasing houseflies with the Shop-Vac.

There are so many flies in my kitchen, a flyswatter only stirs them into whorls, like leaves in an eddy on a fall day. One by one I trap them at the corners of windows and suck them into the hose, like a sandpiper sucking up his dinner. A sandpiper can eat as fast as a hundred and eighty pecks a minute. But I don't think I have that many flies.

I have a jigsaw puzzle of the Tower of Babel. It's nine thousand pieces.

•

When I was little, I helped my dad take inventory at his auto parts store. I sat on the oiled wood floor in the old downtown building for hours and counted bolts, nuts, screws, hoses, and parts of cars.

MaRe had a camellia bush that was infested with bugs. Her friends told her the bush was going to die. Day after day, MaRe went out in the yard and picked all the bugs off the camellias.

When I lived at the cabin, my neighbor Alice, Gene's wife, found a half dozen scrawny kittens covered with fleas. Every day after breakfast, she went outside and sat on the porch, picked up the kittens one by one, laid them upside down in her lap, and pinched off the fleas.

In the yard at the house of steps is a round, dead spot in the grass where for years tenants have been dumping unwanted belongings and setting them on fire. The redbud trees near the spot are charred and dying, and the dirt is deep in rusty nails, hinges, melted glass, fragments of insulation, and bolts as long as my forearm that I can't imagine a use for. Sometimes I sit out there and sift through the dirt, pick out the buried hardware, and put it in trash bags so I can carry it away to the dumpster.

•

Today is the first of August. The day is scorching and the sky is clear. Time to mow, before the next round of thunderstorms rolls in this afternoon. From a white sky, white light burnishes the leaves, polishing them like Japanese tiles as it falls.

Hawk

*T*he summer weekend was sultry when I decided to go on retreat in the yard. I was feeling irrelevant. What was I here for, anyway? Nothing I was doing seemed important. Getting through the days was a monotonous chore, and I was bored with my work and tired of myself.

But Thomas Merton said to plunge into the heart of suffering. So maybe if I sat in the yard on a blanket and fasted and suffered and asked for a vision, I'd get a message. A bolt of lightning. A sign from God. Any old miracle would do, just something to shock me out of my complacency. I had friends who talked to dead relatives, left their bodies and went to Russia for the night, and woke up on the ceiling. I didn't know how long it would take for my revelation, but I figured twenty-four hours without food in Kansas heat would probably do it.

I swept the floors, straightened the clutter in the den, shut off the computer, unplugged the phone, and vowed to keep my mouth shut until a miracle happened. I wouldn't talk to anybody or e-mail Kelly or go to the post office.

I filled a milk jug with tap water, went outside to where the west end of the yard dissolved into meadow, and spread a blanket over the prairie grass near a red cedar. Here I would sit, suffer, and wait for something extraordinary to happen.

Instantly I was miserable. I was hot and thirsty and all I could think about was air-conditioning, Mexican food, and the work I wasn't doing. Max circled on the blanket and then settled into a tight curl and looked at me. Red bounded over and stuck his nose in my ear. Floyd stayed where he was, which was smashed under the propane tank, where it was cold all the time.

I watched buzzards circle overhead, listened to the woodpeckers hammer at the trees, chewed a mint leaf. Small planes flew over, headed for the airport near Lawrence. I struggled to keep from dozing. My bangs were plastered to my forehead, and all over me were bugs—flying bugs, creeping bugs, zinging bugs, biting bugs. The breeze was stiff but inconstant. The air felt like bathwater. My back ached from sitting on the ground, and the top of my head was baking.

I thought: Life's too short to be this uncomfortable. Whatever is wrong with me, I'll get over it.

After an hour, I went back in the house, turned on the TV, and ate the Girl Scout cookies I'd been saving in the freezer.

•

It wasn't long before I started feeling disappointed with myself. I hadn't really tried, after all. I hadn't really been committed. I hadn't done my best. I hadn't *lived up to my potential*.

Besides, I'd have some satisfaction in telling Mom I'd sat on a blanket all weekend in the yard. "Honestly," she'd say, and shake her head.

I smothered myself in bug spray and put ice in a thermos with some water. I was starting over. As a reward for my determination, I treated myself to some cheese and a banana. Then I took the blanket back out to the red cedar tree.

I decided to try standing, rather than sitting. I knew a Dakota Indian once, and he said they stood four days and four nights without food or water when they asked for visions, and they prayed and sang and danced the whole time. I wondered how long I could stand and pray for a vision.

I thought, A conversation with a wolf would be nice. Or maybe the Dalai Lama will show up and offer some wisdom. Or Moses. Maybe even the Virgin Mary. Maybe even . . .

But no. That was asking too much.

It's very hard work, to stand for a long time on a hot day. It's boring, even when you're trying to be reverent and open-hearted and think about sacred things.

After a while, I gave up and sat down. Eventually I grew sleepy and lay down. I dozed. I dreamed about some chickens sitting on a fence telling jokes, and I woke up laughing. Then the crows set up a racket in the woods. A stick fell on my forehead, which made me mad, because it could have put out my eye. I fumed, thinking about sticks, then branches, then trees, and then I thought about climbing trees when I was a girl. I climbed the pecan tree in our front yard and sat on a high limb and watched cars go by on the road; watched Miss Ibba's gardener trim the camellia bushes; watched Miss Mildred, in her fur coat, drive her Cadillac around on her front lawn, picking up trash and tossing it across the street into our yard.

At last a red-tailed hawk flew over, carrying something in her mouth. As she came my way she swooped and then dropped it, and a dark shape fell into the grass near me. I got up and searched around. At the corner of my blanket was a dead baby squirrel.

🏠I was watching an old *Perry Mason* episode one afternoon when a witness told Perry: "A blind man often accuses the whole world of darkness." It reminded me of something a Zen master said to me once. "You're always looking for God. Go sit by the pool and drink a margarita. See."

Cow Zen

Old pond.
A frog jumps in.
The sound of water.

Bashō

Cows. Cows.

Say it like a southerner: *cayows.*

The word is simple, and it comes out round and soft, like the soft-eyed animals it calls to mind. It's poetical, that word *cows,* one of those cases where form echoes content. C-O-O-O-W-S.

Cows. They're never busy; they just are. They stand around in a field all day long chewing, or they wade in a pond, or they lie under a tree. If you walk up to the fence, they back into a knot with their tails touching and their heads sticking out and roll back their eyes and make "mmmmm" sounds in their throats. "MMMMM," they say. "Ommmm."

Cartoonists like cows. Cartoonists draw cows in La-Z-Boys, cows playing bridge, cows standing on hillsides having philosophical conversations. They draw cows driving Mack trucks. They draw cows with halos guarding the Pearly Gates and horny devil-cows in hell. Chick-fil-A cows sell chicken sandwiches, and Gateway 2000 uses computer cows. Steve Martin wrote about cows wearing sunglasses. Renegade cows, he called them.

An English professor I know raises renegade cows on the side. He calls them his wild cows. He once shut them up in his barn, and they got mad and knocked his best saddle off the sawhorse and trampled it flat in the dirt. They like to get out from behind the fence, he says, and climb the hill and stand in the paved road and stop traffic. The sheriff has to come out and direct cars around them until the professor can round up his renegade cows and make them go home.

Sometimes, those renegade cows escape into the woods behind the professor's pond and go off on a rampage. They don't come back for days. Those wild cows, says the professor, shaking his head. They came from Texas.

When I lived in Georgia, Gene, a farmer all his life, told Alice that he ought not to raise cows. "I'm too tender-hearted, Alice," he said.

"Amy, Gene can't hardly stand to sell those cows," Alice told me. "If a cow dies, Gene won't put it out in the woods and let the buzzards get it. He'd rather break his back digging a six-foot hole to bury it in."

The first time Gene had to sell some cows, he made his grandson come and round them up. The second time, he made his son do it. By the third time, he'd run out of grown kids who lived near the farm, and his daughter in Atlanta said she wasn't about to come home to round up cows, so Gene himself had to pick out the cows to sell. Just as he was about to drive the last cow into the trailer, she turned and bolted into the next field.

"I didn't want to sell you nohow," is what Gene told the cow.

Alice also likes cows. She likes the way they look. "Amy, they's just not a thing prettier in this world than a little calf. Now, hogs, I don't like hogs. They just root around and tear up the ground. They make a mess and they smell bad. But cows is so pretty in a field, eating grass. They make me feel peaceful."

🏠 Down the road from the house of steps, my neighbor George has cows. When I jog by his place in the late afternoon, the pastures are dotted with George's black cows with white faces that, through the mist of a hazy summer day, might pass for sheep in a midwestern pastoral poem. Far off in the distance, there might be a young golden-haired shepherd in the field, minding the herd, tapping their behinds with his crook. Later he'd sit under a cottonwood tree and play the flute.

Piping down the valleys wild,
Piping songs of pleasant glee,
Pipe a song about a [cow]—

wrote William Blake. There would be a basket of wild straw-berries by the boy's side, a fox curled up soft and warm at his feet, a meadowlark perched on his shoulder. Because it's Kansas, there would be no wolves to drive away, but there might be a coyote hiding out under the cedars, waiting for twilight.

Several weeks ago I saw a black cow standing on a creek bank straining to eat the leaves on a branch above her reach. I pulled over to watch her struggle. Her neck was stretched straight up, like a giraffe's.

No matter how that cow stretched, she couldn't get to those leaves. They were within inches of her mouth, but no force on earth could have raised her high enough to reach them. Still she kept trying. Sometimes she'd strain so hard she'd lose her balance and stumble forward. Then she'd shake her head, back up, and try again. The other cows didn't pay her the least attention.

A gray tree frog has moved in downstairs. I find him on the bathroom mirror, in the kitchen sink, on the window ledge, and on top of the refrigerator; except once I found him in my Special K, which I'd left in a bowl on the breakfast table while I was making toast.

Watch the frog, Suzuki said. If you touch him, he hops. If something comes along to eat, he sticks out his tongue and snaps it up. He has no idea he's a frog. He's just his plain old froggy self. It's nothing special.

Concert at Full Moon

*We are—we know not what;—light-sparkles
floating in the aether of Deity.*

Thomas Carlyle

$\mathcal{T}$he band is called Talisman, and Sara and Carl and their
friend Russ are the musicians. I'm sitting in the Full Moon
Cafe in downtown Lawrence wrapped up in the scent of
Greek food. I'm listening to Scottish ballads, Swedish love
songs, Finnish waltzes, and I'm dipping hot pita bread into
hummus. I'm drinking a mellow French red wine. Patchouli
incense from the store up front selling Eastern rugs, saris, and
Sherpa bells wafts through the room, blending with the
music and grilled meat that is savory, strong, a little pungent.

Outside, an evening rain drums on awnings and trails
down car windows. Inside the cafe, the lights fall soft on
the wood and native gray stone, the plaster walls and light-
colored tile floors. Where the guests sit, down a step from
the band, the ceilings are low. My waiter is a handsome

blue-eyed boy, lithe and rugged, clad in Levi's and a crisp white shirt. He brings a fragrant candle for my table.

Uncle Walter goes waltzing with bears, sings Sara. Her clear soprano resonates above the men's deep harmonies, the precise notes of Carl's hammered dulcimer, the simple tenor of Russ's classical guitar. Over the break, we share wine. Supper is pasta, feta cheese, sliced tomatoes, Greek salad.

Sara plays the woodwinds and flutes, a recorder, and a drum, a round bowl she sets up on one knee and brushes with a wooden paddle during the Irish marches. The drum sounds out a low, soft *thrum* . . . not like beating, but more sustained.

George dropped by the house of steps one summer morning for a visit. "It's getting so it's hard to neighbor," he said as he sat down. "Our little lives get so involved. You think, well, I've got this to do or that to do."

I've been George's neighbor for two years but I've never seen him except to wave as I jog by his house, and I've talked to his wife Carolyn on the phone a few times. She offered me pumpkins from their garden last fall and a bed in winter when my furnace broke. At Christmas, a card in the mail let me know that in my name she had made a donation to a charity.

At a reading I gave last summer, a man handed me a book to sign and, looking at me intently, said, "It's been a long time. Do you remember me?" He was tall and masculine, slender, wearing cowboy clothes: jeans, boots, long-sleeved shirt, hat. I knew his face, but I couldn't place him in a context. "I helped you move out of a house about fifteen years ago," he said.

"Of course," I said, remembering instantly. His name was Ken. Of all the people who'd promised to help me move that difficult day after my second divorce, some whom I'd known for years, Ken was the only one who came. He'd shown up with his truck and helped me carry things I couldn't possibly have moved by myself. Yet we were only saloon acquaintances who over a course of months had two-stepped together a handful of times, shared a few beers, a few hugs, some laughter.

A mailman in my hometown collects rocks. I was mailing a letter once when he said, "Bring me back a rock."

"A rock?" I said.

"From Kansas," he said.

"What kind of a rock?"

"Any old kind. It don't matter," he said. "Just out of the yard is okay. I got rocks from all over the United States. People bring them to me."

The mailman who delivered the mail to my Georgia cabin now writes me notes on the backs of my forwarded letters. "Hi, Amy!" he writes, with a fancy exclamation point, and signs his initials. When I went running, he'd drive up beside me in his delivery car and offer me ice water from his thermos.

My mail people are always friendly. No matter where I see them delivering the mail, even if it's ten miles from home, they always wave.

A postal clerk I know gave her husband one of her kidneys.

Last October, northeastern Kansas had the second earliest blizzard in recorded Kansas weather history. Elmer called early to say he had a special delivery for me, but I was in class all day. I told him I couldn't get there until after five.

"I'll wait for you," he said. "I'll leave the door open."

Around six, I finally made it to the post office, having slid over miles of snow-covered road past a half dozen pickups in ditches. I rushed in and tore open the envelope. It was my first book contract, the culmination of years of work. Elmer signed as my witness. I believe he was as thrilled as I was.

When Elmer was a boy, his friends Stuff and Mousey nicknamed him Salty. In the fifties, he joined the Marines. Next April Fool's Day, he'll be sixty-eight.

When the Hale-Bopp comet came, Elmer and his wife went out in the fields at night to watch it. But sometimes Elmer takes off on his own. He goes to college football games all over the country, and sneaks into the parties and free buffets as if he were an alum.

Mid-June, after supper. I'm sitting between my friends Roger and Steve on a grassy hill, looking out at the glow on the horizon from Lawrence and Topeka far away. Heat lightning flashes in the north. The moon is out, the night blue.

Fireflies drift and scatter over the fields, tiny reflections of the stars above them.

The night air is cool, and we wrap a blanket around our shoulders. We stay until long after midnight, talking away the hours, bearing the world up in our thoughts and holding it there, examining, wondering, believing. *We are companions,* we say. *We are community.* We endure. Together we weep, we soothe and calm, we rage and laugh and enfold.

Origami Ducks

I wore jeans and a flannel shirt to my first Thanksgiving in Kansas. I was worried that wearing jeans was faintly sacrilegious, even though my friend Penny had said that Thanksgiving was casual at her family's farmhouse in the country. But I grew up in the bowels of South Georgia where Thanksgiving had something to do with Church, and you always wore Sunday Clothes for anything to do with Church.

But I reasoned that even God would wear jeans to a farmhouse Thanksgiving, especially considering that I was taking all of my dogs along to play with Penny's dogs.

I was also taking a traditional dessert: I'd baked from scratch MaRe's two-foot-long chocolate pound cake with penuche icing, to accommodate Penny's large and frequently expanding extended family.

And in gratitude for the invitation to share the holiday, I

took a sack full of origami paper. I wanted to make origami place markers for the dinner table—cranes, flowers, little boxes—graceful, delicate gifts that would complement the decor and please the adults; no doubt whatever children were present would be confined to another part of the house. At MaRe's house in Georgia, Thanksgiving dinner was served in the formal dining room on the best china, with newly polished silver and Big Mama's crystal stemware, individual salt servers, and turkey and pilgrim candles around a silver bowl of pinecones. We children ate at the marble table in the kitchen so we could giggle and tell stories. I had no reason to think things would be different anywhere else.

I've never wanted children because frankly I don't like the noise. But from the minute I walked into that warm Kansas farmhouse, children surrounded me. They were small, loud children. All under the age of six. Like puppies. Eight of them. Looking for something to do. As soon as they saw my origami paper, all my plans for refinement, for delicacy, for a quiet and studied display of my artisanship bellied up like a dead fish and I soon found myself folding ducks because I didn't know how to make turkeys. Every few minutes someone's bold child approached the breakfast table, where I sat amid my piles of papers in every conceivable pattern, color, and size, and pointed with a sticky finger. "I want blue!" the child demanded.

"I want yellow!"

"I want striped!"

"I want a whole family!"

Laughing, Penny set a Bloody Mary in front of me. "I think you're going to need this," she said.

Oh, Lord, I thought. First blue jeans; now vodka. Where I grew up, we used the Thanksgiving wineglasses for sweet tea. Even for Communion, the Blood of the Lamb at the Baptist church was Welch's grape juice.

But I accepted my drink with poise and good humor and kept folding ducks. I made medium-sized cousin ducks, tiny baby ducks, and great big grandmama and granddaddy ducks. They were blue, gold, flowered, foil, plaid, and tie-dyed. Before long, rows of origami ducks began appearing all over the house: under the dining room chairs, behind the sofa, on the counters in the kitchen, where Penny's mom was busy cooking. Occasional visits to the bathroom revealed ducks in the toilet—to see if they would float.

Several Bloody Marys and successively less recognizable ducks later, as the children swirled and eddied around me, I got to thinking that by now, at MaRe's house, the cousins were sprawled in front of the gas fireplace in the living room, playing cards. The Macy's Thanksgiving Day Parade was over, and the ball game had begun, and the fathers and grandfathers were sitting in the den, cheering, while the mothers and grandmothers basted turkey and made sour cream biscuits, squash casserole, sweet potato soufflé, and two gallons of sweet tea, and baked the dressing they'd prepared the day before. They'd be putting dinner out on the cherry sideboard soon, except the biscuits, which they'd set on the table in a silver basket with a linen napkin.

Back in Kansas, at the breakfast table, one of Penny's sisters was using candy corn to turn cupcakes into turkeys. I was teaching the oldest child how to fold flat squares of paper into three-dimensional floating ducks.

At last, far into the afternoon, Penny's dad called the family to dinner. There'd been so many ducks to make that I hadn't made the place markers for the dinner table, so ruefully I was heading for the dining room when Penny called to me. "Oh, not in there, Ame," she said. "Out back."

A supper buffet had seen set up on the glassed-in back porch, and when I came down into that room from inside the house and felt that gray late afternoon calm around me, pressing in through the windows, the out-of-doors pulled me into itself and for a moment I was part of the landscape, just standing in the yard, with the pasture beyond, a few cows, a fat old dog lying beside the barn. The country seemed vacant. It had a windswept sense about it, like a field left fallow too long. I stood at the fence looking west over hay fields and pastures so vast they vanished over the horizon, and I knew there was nothing else out there beyond that fine edge of land where my vision stopped but sand-colored prairies, where the long dry grasses sighed under the cold wind like restless spirits. In the distance, a pheasant, startled by a farm cat, exploded up out of a milo field. Far above in the stillness, vees of geese were winging southward.

Closer in, a crow lighted on a fence post near the barn, and the old dog lifted his head. Around me, Penny's family chattered and laughed, a warm, happy knot of community at the center of a quiet November day.

Inside, a long table covered with green paper was

decorated with big crepe-paper turkeys and a cornucopia of pumpkins and colored ears of corn, and origami ducks waddled in profusion beside the baked beans and Watergate salad. Before we ate, all the people told what they were most grateful for, and all of them included each other. Penny included me. And the day folded itself around me like a blessing.

Afterward, the adults retired to the basement for poker. By midnight I'd won four or five dollars. Then I gathered up my dogs and left.

Back in Georgia, my family was settling into their beds, having worn themselves out picking up pecans in the yard and taking long walks around town and eating leftover-turkey sandwiches for supper. As far as I knew, none of them but me even knew how to play poker, and I surely wouldn't have dared to suggest it.

Coming Round

How great it would be when asked,
"Where do you live?" to be able to reply,
"All over the world."

Soshitsu Sen XV

Garlic has been a cultivated crop for eight millennia, and it can adapt to a new environment in four or five years. I learned this from watching public television.

When I moved to the house of steps, Max wasn't sure he liked it. The first time it snowed, he sat on the deck and refused to budge. He kept examining his paws, as if he didn't know what would happen when he took a step. Maybe, as Suzuki said, he was suffering because he couldn't accept the truth of transiency.

When my family was about to sell our Georgia farm, I had a long conversation with my Uncle Burns about my sadness in losing it. "But you can always return to it, honey," he said, "because it's something you carry inside yourself." Something—an image, a memory, a feeling, an attitude, I think he meant. And although I suspected that what he said was true, still I could not, at the time, separate myself from the part of home I could hold in my hands, put in a vase, walk on and fish in and paddle over.

Besides, I knew the people there, and they were familiar and close and southern, like me.

My friend Beth once wrote that change felt to her like all the loaded cupboards of her psyche falling, and Scott Russell Sanders wrote that people could find harmony in constancy, in staying put. But the paradox is, change is the only constant, and staying put is an illusion.

Still, places have their genius, Wendell Berry says. I discovered the genius of this house by living through the seasons in it—by learning how in fall the leaves crisped and drifted around it, how the trees let in shards of winter light or filtered the summer sunlight into a dusky haze, how they drew shadows like Zen paintings across the walls in the moonlight. I saw where the deer marked out their paths through the woods to the creek, how winter flattened the landscape, how ice hung off the eaves and nestled in the corners of the windows. I heard this house creak and shudder and moan, felt its flurry of drafts, chased its swarms of insects. I felt its bone-cold kitchen floor through the soles of my slippers on mid-winter nights as I hurried to the bathroom.

And I know the people here now, too, and they're familiar and close and midwestern, like me.

•

🏠 The Zen masters say that when one understands that death and life are the same thing, fear ends. Like time, which is not measured by the hands on a clock, like the undercurrents of sound and silence, life and death are ever-present, continuous, unceasing. There is no beginning and no end. There is only being, and all of life is contained within being: all places, all loves, all selves, all homes. This is the truth of transiency.

It was only when I learned I'd never really left home that I understood it had never left me; it had simply expanded to embrace my great awkward leap into the Unexpected. Now I carry inside myself the musk-sweet scent of wild grasses under a red sky, the murmur of a Kansas creek running high after a storm, the sound of migrating geese and the color of pheasants, and they mingle with the low songs of bullfrogs around a Georgia pond, the steady patter of rain in the live oaks outside cabin windows, the fragrance of mimosa, azaleas, jasmine. All of it is home, because *I am* home. I hold home within me; I am the host of the world.

This morning I walked up the driveway and took the rocks out of the mailbox. And thus the year comes round.

🏠 It's Sunday, and after sunset. Winter has lounged into spring, and spring into summer. I'm sitting in the lookout tower, watching for birds in the black walnut tree and the countless other trees behind it, raring their leafy arms against the late August sky. A nuthatch has just flown away, and earlier I saw an indigo bunting on the bird feeder. Tuesday we had such storms the sky turned green, and tornadoes dropped out of the darkness and tore away strips of earth.

But the day is clear now, except for a few bright patches of cloud along the horizon. The dogs lie side by side on the deck and survey the yard like lions, waiting to come in for the night. Soon I will join them, and watch the fireflies sparkle over the yard, lighting the paths that will lead me homeward. Georgia, Kansas, beach, and mountain; cabin, pond, tree house, prairie. I am a pilgrim following paths, I am a pilgrim always coming home.

All ways home.

Always home.

All home.

All home.

I learned this, at least, by my experiment: that if one advances confidently in the direction of his dreams, and endeavors to live the life which he has imagined, he will meet with a success unexpected in common hours. He will put some things behind, will pass an invisible boundary; new, universal, and more liberal laws will begin to establish themselves around and within him; or the old laws be expanded, and interpreted in his favor in a more liberal sense, and he will live with the license of a higher order of beings. In proportion as he simplifies his life, the laws of the universe will appear less complex, and solitude will not be solitude, nor poverty poverty, nor weakness weakness.

H. D. Thoreau,
Walden, or Life in the Woods